Praise for
A Layman's Guide to Metaverse

'I would like to warmly congratulate Kalyanjit & Pratibha on this remarkable accomplishment. They have truly excelled in co-authoring and publishing this very significant book, "*A Layman's Guide to Metaverse.*" Kalyanjit is forever in the forefront of technology. He is an evangelist for new ideas and innovation. He is also my college mate from NIT Kurukshetra and I am very proud of Kalyanjit for having co-authored this important work on Metaverse.

My best wishes and more power to you Kalyanjit & Pratibha.'

Vivek Atray ex IAS
Author of "Finding Success Within" and
TEDx Motivational Speaker

'The content is engaging and provides a solid overview for beginners. It balances technical depth with readability, catering to non-experts while giving enough detail to spark deeper interest. The emphasis on real-world applications, historical context, and emerging challenges makes the book both informative and forward-looking. If you continue refining it with examples and case studies, it could serve as a valuable primer on the metaverse for a wide audience.'

Mawusi Ama Ahiadzi
Ghana

'I compliment the serial Author-Duo, Pratibha and Kalyanjit, for their epic effort in demystifying all we need to know about the mysterious Metaverse, simplifying the complex ecosystem not only for beginners but also for professionals and practitioners. As predicted, by leveraging the emerging technologies like AI and Blockchain, it will become the future of Web—what I would like to call World Wide Wealth. This book is a must-read for all who wish to ride the Internet of Value.'

Dr. Satya N. Gupta
NGNguru, Professor of Practice, South Asian University

'Written in a simple and lucid manner, this book is a handy compendium on the topic for anyone wanting to learn more about Metaverse, its interlinkages with related technologies around it and provides a good insight into use cases in key domains… recommended reading.'

Rajesh Kumar
CMO, Board Advisor, Speaker
https://www.linkedin.com/in/rajeshkjindal

'"*A Layman's Guide to Metaverse*" by Pratibha Das Hatibaruah and Kalyanjit Hatibaruah is an essential read for marketing and business professionals, providing a comprehensive overview of the Metaverse and its implications for the business landscape. The book simplifies complex concepts, making it accessible for those without a technical background, while highlighting how the metaverse can revolutionise marketing strategies, enhance consumer engagement, and create new opportunities for digital commerce. It serves as a valuable resource for understanding the evolving nature of consumer interactions in this emerging digital economy.'

Abhishek Borah
Associate Professor, INSEAD
Author of 'Mine Your Language'

'"*A Layman's Guide To Metaverse*" by Pratibha and Kalyanjit Hatibaruah serves as an excellent introduction to a complex but rapidly evolving technology. Starting with a concise introduction and a clear explanation of the basics, the authors seamlessly guide readers through the key concepts and evolution of the Metaverse. The chapters on Virtual Reality (VR), Augmented Reality (AR), and Mixed Reality (MR) are particularly insightful, providing a comprehensive overview of these immersive technologies and their role in shaping the future of the Metaverse.

The exploration of various Metaverse platforms and environments offers valuable insights into the current state of the Metaverse landscape. The book also effectively highlights the crucial components and enabling technologies, such as blockchain, artificial intelligence, and cloud computing, that underpin the development and usage of the Metaverse, apart from discussing privacy and legal aspects.

Pratibha and Kalyanjit have done an excellent job of explaining various concepts in a way that is easy to understand, avoiding too many technical jargons thus making it accessible to readers with no major prior technical knowledge. The inclusion of real-life pictures showcasing the usage of the Metaverse adds a valuable visual dimension to the book making the concepts more tangible and engaging and helping readers imagine the potential applications of the Metaverse in their own areas.

Overall, a very well-written and informative book. I highly recommend this book to anyone who wants to gain an excellent understanding of the Metaverse without getting bogged down in technical jargons.'

Vijay Sethi
Chairman Mentorkart & Chairman Crafsol Technologies

'Starting from the basics of the attributes contributing in shaping up the Digital Age we are starting to live in today, the authors, with their real-world experience with the technology and the gadgets, have been able to take the reader through a journey which introduces her to MetaHuman, the digital humans you and I can shake hands with today with an unprecedented level of realism. Besides engaging the reader in cognitive exercises in each Chapter, meticulously designed to make the reading remarkably smooth, it happens to be the best part the inclusion of the societal and ethical aspects, without which it would have been incomplete. I congratulate Pratibha-Kalyan, on their ability in integrating talent-skill-360° Sustainable Development Goal approach (rightly doing justice to their names!), and presenting the out-of-the-world technological marvels so lucidly, which ends with that simple yet significant line: "The journey into the metaverse is just beginning, and its future will be shaped by the choices we make today!"'

Eeshankur Saikia
Professor & Head,
Department of Applied Sciences, Gauhati University, Assam, India

'The Metaverse is a concept that demands demystification, and Kalyanjit and Pratibha have done a commendable job in this regard. Their work provides an insightful introduction to a domain that is rapidly reshaping the boundaries of technology, communication, and learning.

In the near future, the ability to navigate and understand various aspects of the Metaverse will be a defining trait of educated and knowledgeable individuals in our society. While numerous books will undoubtedly be written on this vast subject, this one serves as an excellent starting point for beginners and those newly initiated.

The book strikes a fine balance between accessibility and depth—lucid enough for casual, quick reading, yet grounded in authenticity to hold its value for academic purposes. It is a must-read for anyone keen on exploring this transformative space.'

Prakash Chaturvedi
Mumbai, India

'I had the opportunity to read the final draft of *"A Layman's Guide to Metaverse,"* coauthored by Pratibha Hatibaruah and Engineer Kalyan Hatibaruah, as a somewhat perplexed layman who heard the terms and, perhaps, had a bit of vague or naive ideas. The book comprises 17 succinct chapters, which describe the aspects of the phenomenon in simple language. The book definitely had its effect in demystifying the Metaverse. The chapters range from explaining the technology and its application in different fields, from entertainment, communication to education and productivity. The book very aptly covers the challenges involved, if Metaverse is to become the next mass social medium benefitting all, and its potential harms and ethical issues involved. I recommend the book to all who want to keep up to date with emerging technological phenomena that may have far-reaching implications for humanity.'

Dr. Jayanta B Sarma
NHS, UK

'As someone who truly believes in the potential of the Metaverse/immersive experiences, I congratulate my friend Kalyan on his: "*Layman's Guide to Metaverse.*" I am very certain that readers will get the needed clarity on concepts of Extended reality and the Metaverse, whatever your background is. With engaging world examples, this presents a unique yet comprehensive view of the realm of Metaverse.

My best wishes to future Metaverseans.'

Rrahul

'"*A Layman's Guide to Metaverse*" is a book that comes truly close to its name. For a complete novice like me to the IT world whose knowledge of the industry didn't go much beyond the use of Microsoft Office and user friendly apps, the book really demystified the intrigues that I always had for the new verbose jargons like Metaverse, VR, AR etc., and their relative pertinence in the real world. Written in a simple and precise manner in a well structured format, the book takes the reader to the realms of the digital world by unravelling its mystery chapter by chapter. I congratulate the authors of this book for its publication, which will benefit the older and younger generations alike in deciphering the enigmatic world that the Metaverse is!'

Sushil Kumar
Ex-VP(EPC);
Now A Traveller and Writer;
Worked/Lived-Asia/ME/Africa/EU/LAC/N America-Visited 58 nations so far

'*Generation Beta* (those born between 2025 and 2039), will be exposed to a world dominated by advanced technology—virtual reality, augmented reality, artificial intelligence, internet of things etc. Understanding this landscape is crucial in shaping tomorrow's conversations and innovations. Whether you are a curious student, a professional seeking to upskill, an educator, or just a concerned parent wanting to connect better with the next generation, this book serves as an excellent starting point for understanding the technological revolution already underway. I encourage everyone interested in the future to read this as a gateway to understanding emerging technologies.'

Riddhi Shah
Consumer Insights, Sony Pictures Networks India

'"*A Layman's Guide to Metaverse*" by Pratibha Das Hatibaruah and Kalyanjit Hatibaruah provides an accessible introduction to the concept of the metaverse, tracing its evolution from early ideas to its current significance in technology and society. The book simplifies complex topics, making it suitable for readers without a technical background, while emphasising the metaverse's potential to transform social interactions and commerce. It serves as a valuable resource for students, educators, and professionals seeking to understand the implications of this rapidly developing digital landscape.'

Dr Samir Baruah
Former CGM Indian Overseas Bank
Presently:
Adjunct Faculty - Department of MBA, Tezpur University

'I have found the book very useful to understand the world of Metaverse. It's a great book for tech enthusiasts who want to get a thorough understanding of the different features and functionalities offered by Metaverse.

The book effectively describes the metaverse as a virtual space that blends digital and physical realities, utilizing VR, AR, and blockchain technologies. The clear explanations, paired with relatable examples, ensure that readers grasp not only what the Metaverse is but also how it may shape the future of online interactions.

Overall, the guide serves as an excellent starting point for those new to the concept of Metaverse and I would recommend people to buy a copy to keep themselves updated about the new trends going on in the Metaverse.'

Bhairav Phukan
MS Student in Computer Engineering, Columbia University.

'"*A Layman's Guide to Metaverse,*" and I have to say, it's really well-written and thoughtfully put together. I loved how you guys broke down complex topics like blockchain and NFTs into simpler

explanations that someone with no background (like me) could follow. It's clear you've made a big effort to make these ideas accessible, and that really stood out to me.'

Ranju Das
Guwahati, India

A Layman's Guide To Metaverse

By

Pratibha Das Hatibaruah
& Kalyanjit Hatibaruah

Published by Flugel Publishing House

First Edition, January 2025

ISBN: 978-9334179118

Disclaimer

This book aims to provide a foundational understanding of the Metaverse in a simple and engaging manner. While every effort has been made to ensure accuracy, readers should consider this book a guide to exploring the Metaverse rather than a substitute for professional advice where applicable.

Although the authors and publisher have taken all reasonable steps to ensure that the information in this book is accurate at the time of publication, they assume no responsibility for any errors, inaccuracies, omissions, or inconsistencies. The authors and publisher disclaim any liability for any loss, damage, or disruption caused by errors or omissions, whether resulting from negligence, accident, or any other cause.

This book may include references to third-party sources, technologies, and platforms; their inclusion does not imply endorsement or affiliation.

Dedication

♣ To the Present and Future Generations ♣

May you grow up at the forefront of technology, using it not only to advance knowledge but also to bring about positive changes. We hope you foster a deep sense of responsibility towards society, the environment, and the well-being of all. As you navigate the ever-evolving digital world, may your actions be guided by compassion, sustainability, and a commitment to building a better future.

♣ To our children, Ron and Jesse ♣

You bring balance, love, and endless joy to our lives. Your understanding and support have been our guiding light, and we couldn't have asked for anyone better to share this journey with.

Contents

Foreword

by

V.M. Bansal, ***IAS (Retd)***

Chairman, New Delhi Institute of Management

Visionary authors who are experts in the field of Metaverse technology have shared their profound insights and expertise in this book, illuminating the path forward for the Metaverse and its myriad applications in the future of innovation.

From the latest advancements in AI and AR/VR to the exciting possibilities of NFTs and digital twins, this book serves as a comprehensive guide to the future of the Metaverse. The authors adeptly navigate the convergence of blockchain, AI, and AR/VR, unveiling new frontiers in virtual offices, digital twins, and NFTs.

Their work creates a rich tapestry of insights and practical examples that will be indispensable for both the seasoned technologists as well as those curious about the Metaverse.

As the Metaverse continues to evolve, this book offers a thorough roadmap for understanding its transformative potential. It invites readers to explore the innovative applications, economic opportunities, and practical examples presented, providing a clear vision of what lies ahead in this rapidly expanding digital landscape.

With My Best Wishes to the Readers,

V.M. Bansal, ***IAS (Retd)***

Chairman, New Delhi Institute of Management

Advisor to Former Lieutenant Governor, Delhi

Special Invitee, PHDCCI Management Committee & (Ex) Chairman, PHDCCI Education Committee

Special Invitee to Education and Skill Committees of FICCI and ASSOCHAM

On Boards of DMA and Kiwanis Club

Member, AICTE (Government of India), National Steering Committee on Internships, and NITTTR, Government of India

Preface

In today's fast-paced technological landscape, understanding innovations like blockchain, the Metaverse, and other Web3 technologies has become essential. This need spans across various groups—from students exploring career paths to professionals aiming to upskill, and even laypersons trying to keep up with everyday digital tasks. The COVID-19 pandemic starkly highlighted this divide, as non-tech-savvy individuals, including educators, faced challenges adapting to online platforms. Similarly, senior citizens often struggle with digital payments for basic utilities, underlining the necessity for broader digital literacy.

Another example of the critical need for staying updated with technology is seen in small business owners who had to rapidly pivot to online models during the pandemic. Many found themselves grappling with e-commerce platforms, virtual storefronts, and digital customer engagement, which were previously unfamiliar territories. This shift underscored the importance of digital competence in ensuring business continuity and growth.

Drawing from our extensive experience in workshops and classes, we structured this book to address these types of challenges. Some topics are introduced casually within specific chapters to provide immediate context, with deeper explorations reserved for later sections. This approach helps readers engage with the material gradually without feeling overwhelmed. For instance, complex concepts like decentralised ecosystems or virtual economies are introduced with simple analogies before being explored in detail, ensuring a smooth learning curve.

Given the technical nature of the subject, we have striven to maintain clarity and accuracy while using relatable examples, diagrams, and anecdotes to keep the content engaging. While a story-like or overly informal tone may not always be suitable, our focus remains on making these topics as accessible as possible.

We've also taken care to revisit key ideas throughout the book, mirroring our teaching approach. This repetition helps reinforce critical concepts, ensuring readers can retain and connect the dots as they progress. We believe this method prevents readers from feeling overwhelmed, making it easier for them to grasp and internalise foundational ideas about the Metaverse.

We hope this book serves as a valuable resource for a wide audience, offering insights and practical knowledge to navigate the evolving digital world confidently.

Pratibha Das Hatibaruah
Kalyanjit Hatibaruah

Chapter 1
Introduction to the Metaverse
Understanding the Basics

The term metaverse has varied interpretations around the world. Some view it as a digital realm for socialising with friends or maybe a multi-world gaming platform, while others perceive it as a digital marketplace for businesses and clients. It has in fact become a fast-evolving concept calling the attention of not only the tech industry and enterprise leaders but also people from all walks of life, making it almost a household term. Nevertheless, despite all the hype, there is a great deal of vagueness and bewilderment surrounding the term. We get questions about it all the time from acquaintances and peers in the industry as well as those outside, especially centring around its effect, whether it will have a positive or negative impact on humanity. The speculation around it, rather, has a vibe of how the internet was talked about in the 70's and 80's. That was the time when people did not understand what the internet exactly meant and what it looked like or how it was used. In simple words the metaverse embodies the notion of a virtual world that is fully-realised, though one must keep in mind that it is not yet a single entity. In other words, it comprises multiple emerging technologies that enables users to engage with each other and digital objects in a 3D environment. Although it may seem like a futuristic aspiration, technological advancements and the growing prevalence of virtual and augmented reality are bringing the metaverse closer to reality.

Evolution and origins of the Metaverse

In order to gain a better understanding of the metaverse, let us go back in time and look at how the idea of metaverse actually began as well as its evolution over time. The origin of the term "Metaverse" can be traced back to Neal Stephenson's 1992 science fiction novel "Snow Crash," in which he introduced the concept of human avatars and software agents interacting in realistic 3D environments. Digital avatars were used by Stephenson's characters to explore a virtual world and escape their dystopian reality. The novel featured a portrayal of a virtual-reality world with futuristic technologies resembling mobile computing, wireless internet, virtual reality, smartphones, digital currency, and augmented-reality headsets that was remarkably similar to the ones we have today.

However, since the 1990s, there have been tremendous advancements in the fields of AR, VR, and gaming. As a result, the metaverse has come to fruition through the development and progression of basic online games and virtual environments to an interconnected virtual universe. The first online game, "MUD" (Multi-User Dungeon), was created in 1978 and paved the way for other games, such as "Second Life" and "World of Warcraft," which allowed players to create avatars and interact with each other in virtual worlds. The metaverse concept has gained momentum due to advancements in technology, such as virtual and augmented reality, artificial intelligence, and blockchain. The combination of these technologies has made it possible to create a more immersive, interactive, and decentralised virtual world.

To bolster their position at the frontier of these emerging technologies, many companies are embracing the concept of metaverse and envisioning a digital economy that will leverage its features to create, buy, and sell goods. Tech giants like Microsoft, Apple, Nvidia, Unity, Roblox and Google are investing heavily to bring this vision to life. As investors and businesses seek to capitalise on what could be the next major trend, interest in the metaverse has grown significantly.

Meanwhile, in an effort to position his company as a front-runner in metaverse development, Mark Zuckerberg, CEO of Facebook, took a significant step by rebranding the corporation's identity to Meta in July 2020, effectively turning it into a household buzzword. Besides the big tech companies there are numerous small companies and startups that are combining these emerging technologies with innovative ideas to create complex virtual environments and enable users to interact in newer, exciting ways. Enhanced brand recognition, customer engagement, and the discovery of fresh revenue streams are other key reasons why even non-tech companies are venturing into the metaverse space.

What is the Metaverse?

The metaverse is a term that has been used to describe a hypothetical virtual world where people can interact with each other and digital objects in a fully-realised three-dimensional environment. It is essentially a collective virtual space that can be accessed by anyone, anywhere in the world. It goes beyond the confines of traditional online interactions, offering a fully-immersive experience where users can engage in a variety of activities such as socialising, working, shopping, and entertainment. It is a shared virtual space where users can interact with each other and digital objects in a way that is more natural and intuitive than traditional online interactions. In its most basic sense, the metaverse can be understood as a successor to today's mobile internet and social networks. It aims to provide deeper immersion and embodiment compared to our current 2D experiences on phones and computers.

One of the key components of the metaverse is the use of virtual and augmented reality technologies. Virtual reality (VR) refers to a completely immersive experience where the user is transported to a digital world, while augmented reality (AR) overlays digital content onto the real world. Both technologies are essential for creating a fully-realised metaverse experience where users can interact with digital objects and each other in a seamless way.

Simply put, the metaverse is a network of interconnected 3D virtual worlds that exists alongside our physical reality, utilising social media concepts to foster social connections. It can be defined as a simulated digital environment that employs technologies such as head-mounted displays (HMDs), an AR cloud, the Internet of Things (IoT), 5G, artificial intelligence (AI), and spatial technologies to create virtual spaces for users to engage with each other in ways that emulate real-life interactions. Unlike typical digital content consumption, the user experience in these online spaces is multidimensional and unconstrained by physical limitations. Instead, it offers an immersive, persistent, and three-dimensional digital experience that blends the physical and digital worlds, allowing users to fully immerse themselves in a space where the two merge. The metaverse not only allows users to consume content but also to become part of it through augmented reality spaces, which overlay visual elements, sound, and other sensory input onto real-world settings. In this way, objects from the virtual world are projected into the real world via screens to enhance the user experience. Meanwhile, virtual reality allows people to interact socially and professionally using their 3D avatars. This means that individuals can connect, work, play, build communities, buy and sell items, invest in currency, take classes, travel, and enjoy immersive content in 3D virtual reality.

Another crucial aspect of the metaverse is the use of blockchain technology. Blockchain is a decentralised ledger that allows for secure transactions and the creation of digital assets. In the metaverse, blockchain can be used to create a virtual economy0 where users can buy, sell, and trade digital assets such as virtual real estate, clothing, and other virtual goods. This creates a new kind of economy that is not limited by physical boundaries.

The potential of the metaverse is vast and multifaceted. It has the potential to transform the way we work, offering a virtual office space where employees can collaborate in real-time regardless of their physical location. It can also revolutionise the way we shop, offering a fully-immersive online shopping experience where users can try on virtual clothing and accessories. The metaverse can also transform the way we socialise, offering a new kind of online community where users can interact with each other in a more natural and immersive way. This opens up new possibilities for social interaction, from virtual meetups and networking events to collaborative workspaces and virtual classrooms.

However, the metaverse also raises several concerns, particularly around privacy and ownership. In a fully-realised virtual world, users may have to relinquish some of their privacy in order to fully participate. There is also the question of who owns the virtual assets created within the metaverse. As with any new technology, there are both benefits and risks, and it will be important to address these concerns as the metaverse continues to develop.

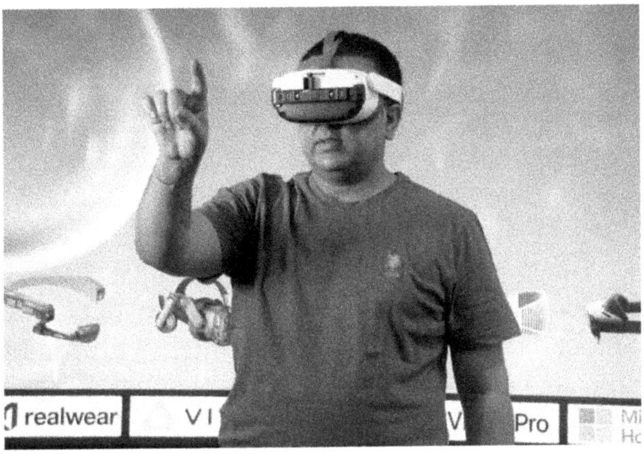

Exploring a metaverse application (Picture credit – Metaverse911)

Core characteristics of the metaverse include:

· **Persistence** - The metaverse is always "on" much like how the internet exists perpetually. Virtual worlds and digital assets exist beyond a single experience or moment.

· **Interoperability** - Content, identities, payments, and more can flow between metaverse experiences across platforms, unlocking network effects.

· **Accessibility** - Open access and low barriers allow broad, global usage across devices from smartphones to headsets. High-speed broadband and 5G expand access.

· **Presence** - Users feel a sense of embodied presence, as if they are inside a virtual world through digital avatars. Spatial audio, haptics, and extended reality hardware deepen immersion.

- **Embodiment** - Users are represented as full-body 3D digital avatars that are persistently identifiable across worlds. Avatars represent identity and enable social engagement.
- **Economies** - Virtual economic systems, digital goods, cryptocurrencies, NFTs, and blockchain enable user creations to hold real value. New economic opportunities arise.
- **Autonomy** - Individuals have agency over their experiences, identities, content, and privacy within decentralised metaverse networks.

The significance of the metaverse extends far beyond mere entertainment or escapism. It has the potential to revolutionise how we communicate, collaborate, learn, work, and conduct business. In the metaverse, distance becomes irrelevant, allowing individuals from across the globe to connect and collaborate in real-time. It opens up new avenues for creativity, innovation, and expression, empowering users to bring their ideas and visions to life in ways that were previously unimaginable.

Moreover, the metaverse presents exciting opportunities for economic growth and development. Virtual economies, powered by cryptocurrencies, non-fungible tokens (NFTs), and blockchain technology, are flourishing within the metaverse. These digital economies enable new forms of commerce, trade, and ownership, paving the way for innovative business models and revenue streams.

While it is still in its early stages of development, advancements in virtual and augmented reality, as well as blockchain technology, are bringing us closer to a fully-realised metaverse experience. The metaverse marks a transformative change in our perceiving and engaging with digital technology. It is a vast, interconnected digital universe that offers boundless opportunities for exploration, collaboration, and innovation. As with any new technology, it is important to approach the metaverse with caution and address any concerns around privacy and ownership. However, the potential benefits of the metaverse are too great to ignore, and it is an exciting time to be at the forefront of this emerging technology. With vision, creativity, and collective effort, the metaverse has the potential to transform our world in ways that we have yet to fully comprehend.

Meta Horizon Workrooms (Picture credit - Meta)

Workrooms is an immersive way to meet teammates, brainstorm ideas, share presentations and get things done, whether you're joining in virtual reality or from a regular video call.

Chapter 2
The Concept and Evolution of the Metaverse

The metaverse is a term that's gained widespread popularity in recent years, but its roots stretch back decades. The concept of a virtual world where users can interact with each other and digital content has been explored in various forms of media, from books and movies to video games and virtual reality experiences. However, the idea of the metaverse as we know it today has its origins in the early days of the internet. In this chapter, we will delve deeper into the origins and development of the metaverse, exploring influential works of fiction, key technological milestones, and major developments that have shaped the concept over time.

The origins of the metaverse concept trace back to pioneering virtual reality (VR) research in the 1980s, where scientists envisioned advanced telepresence applications using head-mounted displays and haptic bodysuits to create embodied virtual experiences. In fact, both in the 1980s and 1990s, as the internet began to take shape, researchers and technologists began to envision a more immersive and interactive digital environment. They imagined a space where users could move freely between different virtual worlds, interact with other users, and create and manipulate digital objects. This vision of a collective virtual space, where the boundaries between the physical and digital worlds blur, laid the foundation for what would later be known as the metaverse. However, the bulky hardware of the time was too limited for mass adoption.

Author Neal Stephenson's 1992 dystopian novel "Snow Crash" popularised the term "metaverse" for an immersive, life-like 3D virtual reality space called the Street accessed by billions where people escape their harsh physical realities. This vision seeded grand ideas of alternate worlds interconnected with physical spaces.

Drawing inspiration from "Snow Crash," other authors, such as William Gibson's "Neuromancer" and Orson Scott Card's "Ender's

Game," further popularised the idea of a virtual realm where people could transcend physical limitations and explore endless possibilities. These works influenced subsequent discussions and initiatives in the technology community.

Technological Milestones

While the metaverse initially existed as a fictional concept, technological advancements have gradually transformed it into a tangible reality. One of the key milestones was the development of virtual reality (VR) and augmented reality (AR) technologies. The advent of VR and AR technologies paved the way for the evolution of the metaverse. With the introduction of VR headsets, such as the Oculus Rift and HTC Vive, users could immerse themselves in digital environments and interact with them in unprecedented ways.

In the early 2000s, Linden Lab's "Second Life" and World of Warcraft games created buzz for letting users build entire virtual economies, social networks, and even conduct business. By 2013, over a million people inhabited this early rendition of interconnected 3D worlds. Tabletop role playing games like "Dungeons and Dragons" also brought metaverse-like worldbuilding to mass audiences.

The rise of multiplayer worlds really took off in the 2010s with games like Roblox, Fortnite, and Minecraft that let kids create, own, trade, and monetise in-game assets using real money. Huge virtual concerts hosted in these environments previewed future visions. High speed 5G internet and affordable VR headsets then unlocked more immersive user experiences.

Facebook was the first to make a major metaverse push by acquiring VR headset maker Oculus in 2014. This investment into lifelike avatars, hand tracking, and pass through mixed reality glasses seeds Facebook Horizon and other social VR spaces today. Other big tech firms like Microsoft, Google, and Apple have since accelerated metaverse development through hardware and software breakthroughs.

Major Developments in the Concept

As technology continued to advance, so did the concept of the metaverse. Perhaps most profoundly, blockchain technology introduced by Bitcoin in 2008 brought concepts of persistent digital ownership, decentralised authority, and token-based economics to virtual worlds for the first time. Combined with smart contracts, crypto wallets and digital collectibles like NFTs, entire creator economies are now thriving in metaverse environments powered by Web3 infrastructure.

Major investments from gaming giants like Epic Games and Unity now enable developers to rapidly build expansive, interconnected 3D worlds using powerful game engines, easy drag and drop tools, and templates for everything from architecture to clothing design. The pieces are primed for the next generation internet – an immersive spatial web fundamentally different from the flat web of today.

Another crucial development was the emergence of metaverse platforms and environments. Companies like Decentraland, Cryptovoxels, and Somnium Space created expansive virtual worlds with diverse landscapes, allowing users to build, trade, and interact with each other. These platforms symbolise the shift from isolated virtual experiences to a connected metaverse ecosystem.

Today, the metaverse is a reality, with a wide range of virtual worlds, platforms, and experiences available to users. From virtual reality games and social networks to immersive art installations and virtual concerts, the metaverse offers a diverse and ever-expanding array of experiences. And with the continued advancement of technology, the possibilities for the metaverse are only limited by our imagination.

The Future of the Metaverse

The concept of the metaverse holds vast potential for both individuals and businesses. It presents opportunities for immersive user experiences, social interactions, virtual economies, and innovative applications in various domains such as education, healthcare, and art. However, challenges remain, particularly in areas of privacy, security, and interoperability.

As technology continues to advance, the metaverse will likely become increasingly integrated into our daily lives. Interoperability among different platforms and standards will play a vital role in ensuring seamless communication and interaction between various virtual environments. Legal and ethical considerations will also be essential in shaping the metaverse's future, addressing issues such as intellectual property rights, digital identity, and online safety.

Current building blocks leading us toward this future include:

- Omnipresent high-bandwidth 5G and fibre optic communication networks to transmit massive amounts of data across the spatial web and to edge devices like VR headsets.

- High resolution mixed reality displays that blend and augment physical spaces with digital imagery and information.

- Blockchain wallets, crypto payments and NFTs to enable fluid economies where users truly own their digital goods and creations.

- Real-time, photorealistic 3D rendering technologies for embodied user representations through personalised avatars and digital twins.

- Edge computing infrastructure and artificial intelligence algorithms that enable natural user interactions using gesture, voice and even thoughts.

Conclusion

The concept and evolution of the metaverse have come a long way since its inception in science fiction literature. Advances in technology and the increasing interest and investment in virtual worlds have transformed this once-fictitious idea into a tangible reality.

The metaverse holds immense promise, offering boundless opportunities for immersive experiences, virtual economies, and new forms of social interaction. However, realising this vision requires collaboration among technology companies, policymakers, and users to address challenges and ensure the metaverse's ethical and inclusive development.

As we navigate the evolving landscape of the metaverse, it is crucial to remain mindful of its potential impact on society. By harnessing its power responsibly, we can forge a vibrant and interconnected virtual realm that enhances our lives and pushes the boundaries of human imagination.

While expectations and visions for the metaverse vary wildly across optimists and critics, the one irrefutable truth is that many transformative technologies are now mature enough to make this Web 3.0 future feel tantalisingly close.

Chapter 3

Virtual Reality (VR), Augmented Reality (AR), and Mixed Reality (MR)

In the realm of technology, Virtual Reality (VR), Augmented Reality (AR), and Mixed Reality (MR) have taken centre stage. These immersive technologies have the power to transform how we perceive and interact with the world around us. In this chapter, we will delve into the intricacies of VR, AR, and MR, understanding their definitions, applications, and the impact they have on various industries.

Defining Virtual Reality (VR)

Virtual reality (VR) is a technology that immerses users in a completely digital environment, simulating a realistic and interactive experience. It refers to a computer-generated simulation of a three-dimensional environment that can be explored and interacted with by a person. The user typically wears a VR headset that covers the eyes, immersing them in a virtual world that is designed to mimic real-world experiences or create entirely new ones. The use of a headset or goggles completely blocks out the physical world and replaces it with a virtual one. Users can interact with this virtual environment using specialised controllers or hand-tracking technology, allowing them to move, manipulate objects, and engage with digital content in real-time. VR shuts out the physical world by displaying synthetic images and sounds through a headset with sensors tracking the user's movements. VR often includes elements like 360-degree videos, realistic graphics, spatial audio, and haptic feedback to enhance the immersion.

One of the key features of VR is its ability to transport users to different places and experiences, from the depths of the ocean to the surface of Mars. VR is commonly used in gaming, entertainment, and simulation training, allowing users to explore new worlds and scenarios in a safe and controlled environment. It's also used in healthcare for pain management, therapy, and medical training, as well as in architecture and design for virtual walkthroughs and visualisations.

Using VR, you can seemingly step inside fantastical landscapes, play immersive games, attend virtual events or meetings, and interact with objects that don't exist in reality. VR simulations aim to deceive your senses and trick your brain into believing the artificial environment is real.

How VR Works

VR systems typically consist of a headset, motion tracking sensors, and hand controllers. The headset tracks the user's head movements, adjusting the display accordingly to create a seamless and immersive experience. Motion tracking sensors capture the user's body movements, allowing them to interact with objects in the virtual environment.

The Applications and Impact of VR

VR holds vast potential across numerous industries. In gaming and entertainment, VR enables players to dive into realistic and highly immersive experiences, transporting them to virtual realms that were previously unimaginable. VR gaming has gained significant popularity, offering players a fully immersive and interactive experience. It also has potential in various entertainment sectors, such as virtual concerts, movies, and theme park attractions.

Additionally, VR is being utilised for training and education, providing practical simulations for medical professionals, pilots, and engineers to practise their skills in a safe and controlled environment. It also holds promise in educational settings, providing interactive and engaging learning experiences.

In the world of architecture and design, VR allows clients to visualise buildings and spaces before they are constructed, providing a heightened sense of presence and understanding. In psychology and therapy, VR has been used to simulate scenarios to treat anxieties, phobias, and post-traumatic stress disorders. Moreover, VR has the power to transport individuals to places they may never have the chance to visit physically, fostering empathy and understanding.

Key components of VR include:

- VR headset with high-resolution stereoscopic displays for each eye

- Tracking sensors for motion detection and 6 degrees of freedom

- Specialised graphics processing hardware and rendering engines

- Input devices like handheld controllers, haptic vests, omnidirectional treadmills

- Spatial audio systems for 3D sound effects

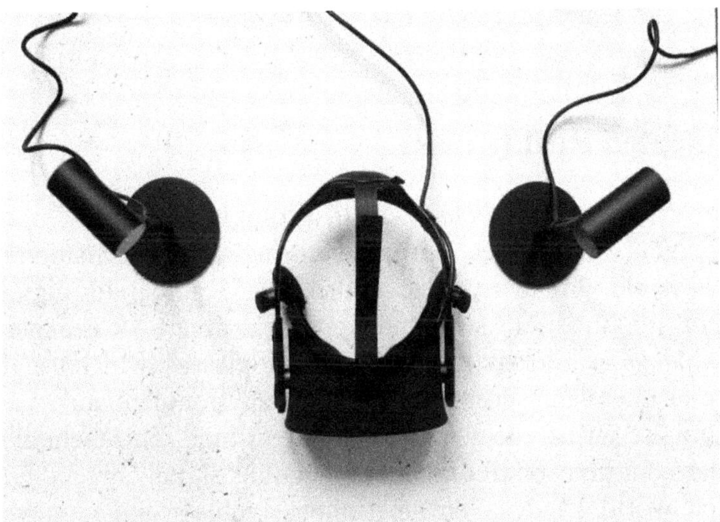

Oculus Rift CV1 VR Headset with Constellation Sensors

Child playing VR games

Augmented Reality (AR)

Unlike VR, which immerses users in a completely virtual environment, Augmented Reality overlays digital information onto the real world. In other words, unlike VR, AR integrates digital elements into the user's surroundings in real-time. AR is experienced through devices like smartphones or smart glasses, which use the device's camera and sensors to detect the environment and superimpose virtual elements onto it in real-time. This technology enhances our perception of reality by adding digital content to the physical world. Devices like smartphones, tablets, and augmented reality glasses offer different ways to engage with AR content.

Augmented Reality in google maps. Using google lens app for augmented reality experience of Eiffel Tower, Paris, France

The Applications and Impact of AR

AR has a wide range of applications across various industries, from gaming and entertainment to education and retail. In gaming, AR games like Pokemon Go and Harry Potter: Wizards Unite have become hugely popular, allowing players to interact with virtual characters and objects in the real world. It also enables immersive experiences in museums, art galleries, and live events, enhancing visitor engagement.

In the retail industry, AR is used to enable customers to visualise how furniture or clothing will look in their homes or on themselves before making a purchase. It is transforming the retail industry by allowing customers to virtually try on products or access additional information about a product through interactive digital overlays.

In education, AR apps can provide interactive learning experiences, allowing students to explore historical sites, dissect virtual organisms, and visualise complex concepts.

AR also has applications in fields such as healthcare, where surgeons can utilise AR overlays to provide real-time guidance during complex procedures. In education, AR is being utilised to enhance learning experiences by overlaying supplementary information onto textbooks or physical objects, making learning more interactive and engaging.

How AR Works

AR technology relies on devices such as smartphones, tablets, or smart glasses to overlay digital content onto the real world. By using the device's camera and sensors, AR applications recognise the physical environment and superimpose relevant information or virtual objects onto the user's view.

Key AR technology components:

- Cameras and depth sensors to scan the environment

- Sophisticated computer vision algorithms to map the world

- Powerful mobile processors and GPUs for rendering

- Spatial tracking to pinpoint locations for anchoring AR objects

- Input methods like gaze tracking, gesture controls, voice commands

Mixed Reality (MR)

Mixed reality (MR) is a blend of both virtual reality (VR) and augmented reality (AR), combining elements of both technologies to create immersive and interactive experiences. MR allows digital content to interact with and respond to the physical environment, creating a seamless integration between the virtual and real worlds. MR devices, such as Microsoft's HoloLens, combine the real-time understanding of the physical environment with the ability to overlay virtual content.

One of the key features of MR is its ability to anchor virtual objects to specific locations in the physical world, allowing users to interact with them in a more natural and intuitive way. MR experiences can be viewed through specialised headsets or glasses, which overlay digital content onto the user's field of view.

The Applications and Impact of MR

MR has a wide range of applications across various industries, from gaming and entertainment to engineering and manufacturing. In gaming, MR experiences can provide more immersive and interactive gameplay, allowing players to interact with virtual objects and characters in the real world.

MR technology enables architects and designers to visualise and manipulate virtual models in real-time within the physical environment. This aids in the design process and improves communication between stakeholders.

In engineering and manufacturing, MR can be used for virtual prototyping, allowing designers to visualise and test product designs in a real-world context. In healthcare, MR can support surgeons by visualising medical images directly onto a patient's body during surgery. Furthermore, MR has implications for collaborative work, enabling remote teams to interact and share virtual content while feeling a sense of presence. It also enables remote consultations and collaboration among healthcare professionals.

How MR Works

MR systems use advanced sensors and cameras to accurately map the physical environment and track the user's movements. This enables virtual objects to be anchored to specific locations in the real world, creating a more immersive and interactive experience.

Key MR capabilities:

- Real-time 3D mapping and spatial awareness of environments

- Object recognition and tracking for precise anchoring

- Hand/body gesture sensing and motion tracking

- Eye tracking and spatial audio for realistic experiences

- Powerful rendering engines for photorealistic visuals

- Head-mounted displays with high-resolution passthrough cameras

Conclusion

Virtual Reality, Augmented Reality, and Mixed Reality represent transformative technologies that have the potential to reshape various industries and enhance human experiences. These immersive technologies enable us to explore new worlds, learn in interactive ways, and connect more deeply with our surroundings.

As VR, AR, and MR continue to evolve, the boundaries between the physical and digital realms will fade, giving rise to an entirely new way of perceiving and interacting with the world. The adoption of these technologies will require careful consideration, addressing challenges such as user experience, privacy, and ethical implications. Nevertheless, these immersive technologies hold immense promise, revolutionising how we work, play, learn, and connect in the future.

Chapter 4

Metaverse Platforms and Environments

The concept of the metaverse has gained significant attention in recent years, as the demand for immersive virtual experiences continues to rise. To bring the metaverse to life, various platforms and environments have emerged, offering users the opportunity to explore, create, and interact within expansive virtual worlds. In this chapter, we will delve into the intricacies of metaverse platforms and environments, examining their key features, notable examples, and the implications they hold for the future of the metaverse.

Defining Metaverse Platforms

Metaverse platforms are digital spaces that serve as the foundation for the metaverse experience. They are the gateways to accessing the vast virtual universe. These platforms provide the infrastructure and tools for users to create, explore, monetise, trade, and engage with virtual content and other users. They often incorporate elements of virtual reality (VR), augmented reality (AR), and blockchain technology to ensure immersive experiences and decentralised interactions. From gaming to socialising, metaverse platforms are revolutionising the way we engage with digital content.

Key Features of Metaverse Platforms

1. **Virtual Worlds**: Metaverse platforms offer vast virtual worlds that users can explore and inhabit. These worlds are characterised by diverse landscapes, ranging from realistic cities to fantastical realms, providing opportunities for endless exploration.

2. **User-generated Content**: Metaverse platforms empower users to create and contribute to the virtual world. Whether it's building structures, designing avatars, or programming interactive experiences, users play an active role in shaping the metaverse environment.

3. **Social Interactions**: Metaverse platforms prioritise social interactions, fostering connections and collaborations between users. They provide avenues for communication, virtual events, and shared experiences, bringing people together irrespective of geographical limitations.

4. **Virtual Economies**: Metaverse platforms often incorporate digital currencies and NFTs (non-fungible tokens) to enable virtual economies. Users can buy, sell, and trade virtual assets, creating unique marketplaces within the metaverse.

Notable Metaverse Platforms

1. **Decentraland**: Decentraland is a decentralised virtual world built on the Ethereum blockchain. It allows users to create, explore, and monetise their virtual experiences. Users can buy and sell virtual land, create and trade digital assets, and interact with others in a virtual environment. It offers a decentralised governance model and enables true ownership of digital assets through the use of blockchain technology.

   Users can buy land parcels represented as NFTs, build apps and experiences, host events, and trade digital assets/wearables - all governed by a DAO (Decentralised Autonomous Organization).

2. **Cryptovoxels**: Cryptovoxels is another metaverse platform built on the Ethereum blockchain, offering users an expansive virtual world to explore and build upon. It is a voxel-based metaverse where users can buy, sell, and build on virtual land. It leverages Ethereum and voxel-based graphics to create a visually distinctive metaverse environment. Cryptovoxels focuses on social interactions and creative expression, allowing users to explore and interact with each other's creations.

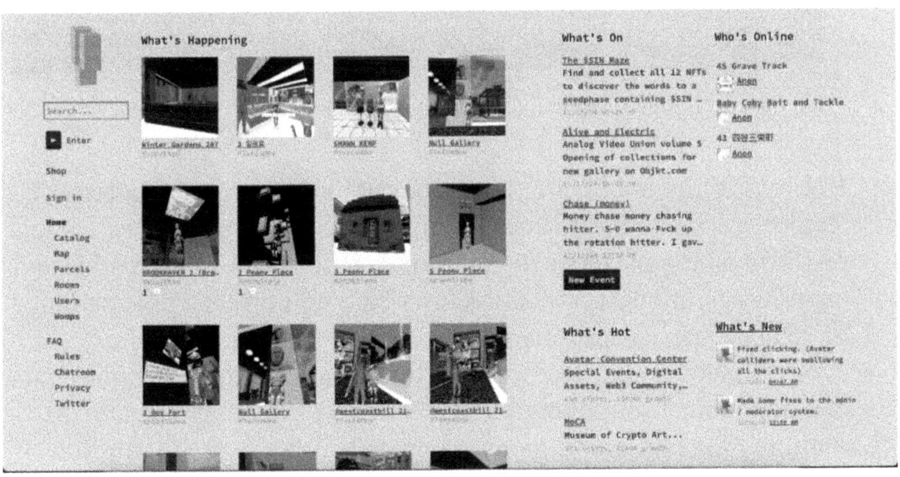

3. **Somnium Space**: Somnium Space is a groundbreaking metaverse platform that redefines the possibilities of virtual reality. It offers users an extraordinary immersive experience within a vast interconnected universe, where they can explore stunning landscapes and engage in interactive encounters with others. What sets Somnium Space apart is its integration of blockchain technology, ensuring secure ownership and transparent transactions of virtual land and assets. This empowers users to create and monetise their digital creations, giving them a sense of ownership and control within the metaverse.

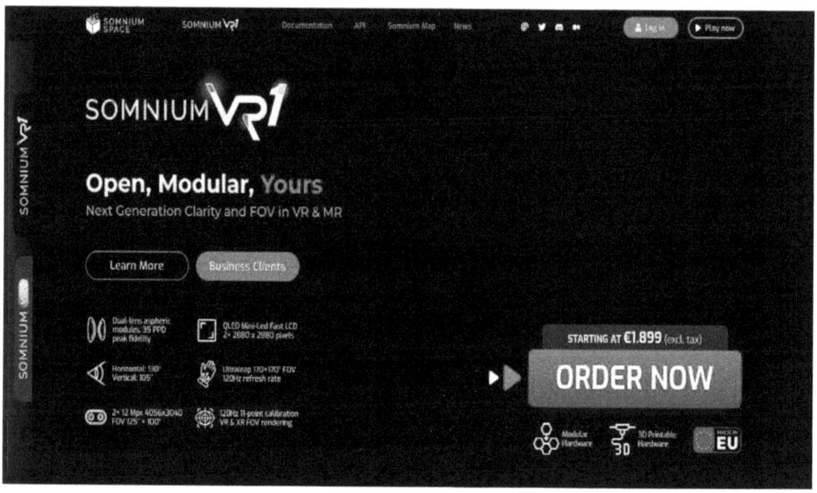

4. **Roblox**: While not explicitly positioned as a metaverse platform, Roblox has gained significant popularity as a user-generated content platform where players can create and share their virtual worlds and experiences. It boasts a massive user base and offers a diverse range of virtual experiences, often created by the community. It has evolved into a co-experience metaverse platform that combines game creation tools, user-generated 3D worlds, social hangouts, and an economy for creators to monetise content. With over 200 million

monthly users, Roblox's blocky aesthetic may seem rudimentary but it leverages persistent spaces, avatars, and ownership.

5. **Sandbox**: The Sandbox is a user-generated content platform where users can create, share, and monetise their own virtual experiences. It uses blockchain technology and non-fungible tokens (NFTs) to enable ownership and trading of virtual assets. Users can build games, virtual worlds, and interactive experiences within the sandbox.

The play-to-earn model allows creators to monetise and profit from their voxel creations. They can create voxel assets using Voxedit, import and sell them on the marketplace as NFTs. Additionally, creators can build and monetise games using the Game Maker tool.

6. **Second Life**: Second Life is a pioneering virtual world that has captivated users since its launch in 2003. It offers a rich and immersive experience, where users can create and explore a vast digital universe. One of Second Life's key strengths is its vibrant and diverse community, which provides a platform for users to connect, socialise, and engage in a wide range of activities. The platform's user-driven economy allows users to buy, sell, and trade virtual goods and services, creating a thriving marketplace where creativity is rewarded. Second Life also provides extensive customization options, enabling users to create unique avatars and design personalised virtual spaces. Furthermore, Second Life values user empowerment and respects intellectual property rights, ensuring that users have full control and ownership over their creations.

7. **Fortnite**: Fortnite is an immensely popular online multiplayer game that has taken the gaming world by storm. Since its release, it has

captivated players with its unique blend of fast-paced action, strategic gameplay, and vibrant graphics. With its ever-evolving map and exciting gameplay modes, Fortnite offers an immersive experience where players can engage in thrilling battles and showcase their skills. One of Fortnite's standout features is its constant updates and collaborations, which keep the game fresh and exciting. The game's dedicated community fosters a sense of camaraderie and competition, as players connect, socialise, and form teams to conquer the virtual battlegrounds. With its captivating gameplay and dynamic community, Fortnite continues to be a dominant force in the gaming industry, attracting millions of players worldwide.

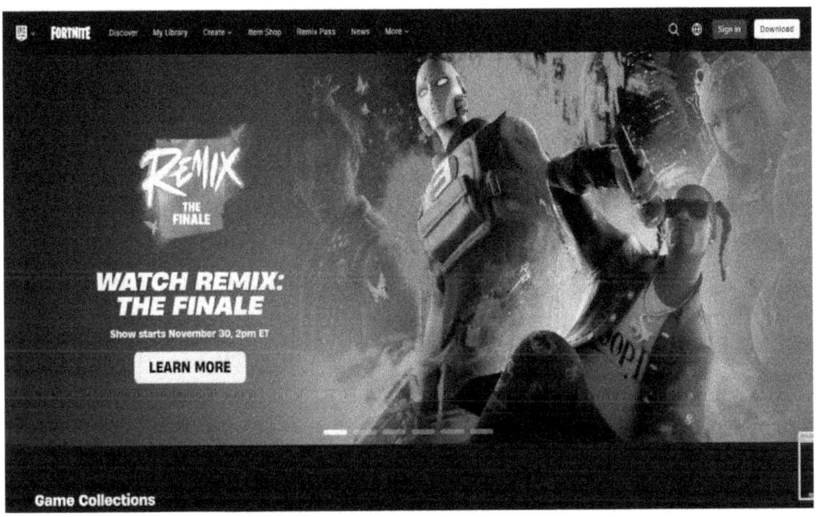

8. **Axie Infinity**: Axie Infinity is an innovative blockchain-based game that transports players into a fantastical world filled with flying robots, magical creatures, mutants, and incredible beasts. Within this immersive environment, players have the ability to breed and raise their own digital pets known as Axies. These adorable creatures serve as companions in battles and wars, as well as vital assets for

expanding and defending the player's universe. By harnessing the power of blockchain technology, Axie Infinity creates a complex in-game economy that has propelled its popularity, establishing it as one of the leading metaverse platforms with gaming applications.

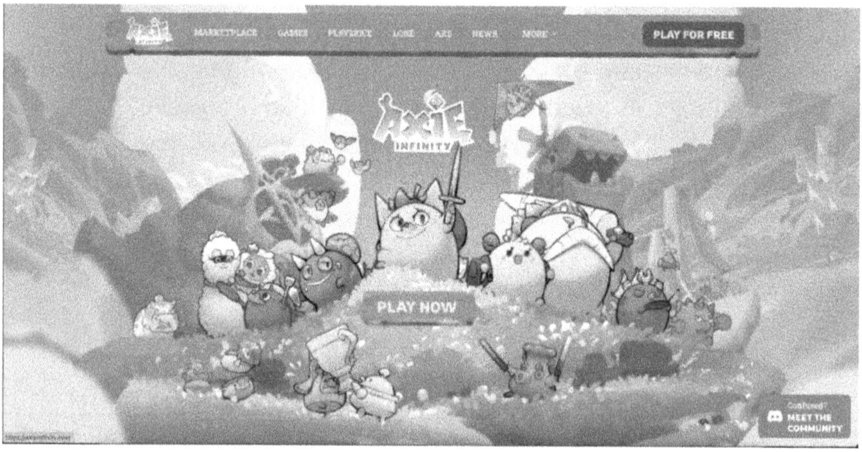

9. **Bloktopia**: Step into the virtual realm of Bloktopia, a captivating 3D metaverse designed as a towering skyscraper with an impressive 21 levels. This unique environment features virtual real estate blocks that users can purchase, each designated with specific spaces meticulously outlined in the floor plan. Transactions within Bloktopia are facilitated by its native currency, BLOK. Powered by the Polygon Network, this cutting-edge platform offers a wide range of opportunities for users to generate revenue through engaging virtual experiences. Whether through immersive games, advertising revenues, real estate ownership, or other innovative avenues, Bloktopia invites users to unleash their creativity, participate in social activities, explore the world of cryptocurrency, acquire virtual real estate, and even attend promoted events within its virtual auditorium.

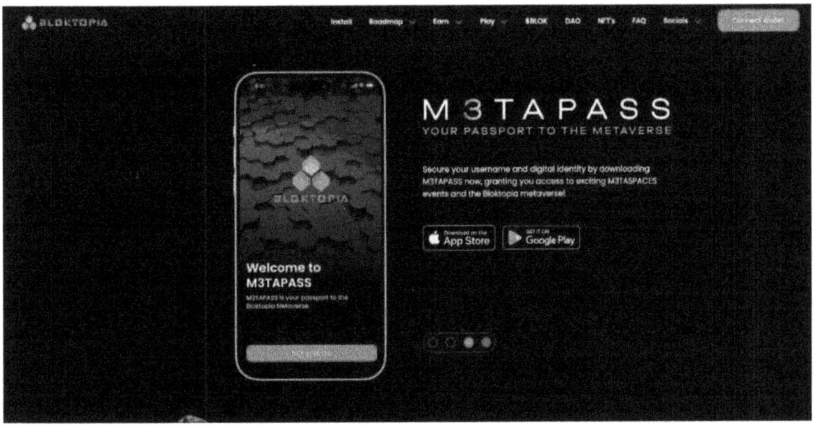

More recently, platforms like VRChat, AltspaceVR, and Sinculife have emerged catering to VR enthusiasts. These immersive social platforms let users hang out with friends or strangers in a variety of imagined 3D worlds deploying expressive customizable avatars.

While basic, these virtual worlds showcase the social connection and self-directed exploration hallmarks of the metaverse. They allow uninhibited identity expression through avatars in malleable shared spaces.

Extending further into connectivity tools, Social VR platforms blend virtual worlds with productivity applications like meeting rooms, virtual offices, classrooms, and events spaces. They aim to replicate real world venues in a virtual context.

Meta's Horizon Workrooms provides VR meeting spaces with virtual whiteboards, document sharing, and spatial audio. Similarly, Mesh for Microsoft lets colleagues interact in mixed reality through customised avatars.

Platforms like Engage, Virbela, and MootUp facilitate virtual conferences, trade shows, networking events, and campuses in customizable VR spaces. Immersive social VR makes remote collaboration and learning more engaging by providing a sense of presence.

VR/AR Creation Tools

To build out these virtual platforms and metaverse experiences, increasingly sophisticated development tools are emerging. Leading game engines like Unity and Unreal provide the core infrastructure for creating dynamic 3D virtual worlds and enabling immersive experiences.

MetaHuman Creator is a free, cloud-based tool that allows users to create realistic digital humans. It's a product of Epic Games and is available within Unreal Engine

Built-in world compositing features, multiplayer functionality, physics engines, animation tools, and real-time ray tracing help creators mock complex environments. Procedural world generation tools from Nvidia automate creation of expansive virtual terrains and landscapes.

On the AR front, platforms like Snap's LenStudio let creators build AR lenses and effects tied to their environment. Apple's ARKit, Google's ARCore and Magic Leap Helio enable development of spatial computing apps that overlay data onto physical surroundings.

Tools like Gravity Sketch and Sprill let designers intuitively create, manipulate and iterate on 3D shapes and environments using VR interfaces and gestures. As the metaverse evolves, more natural virtual design flows will be critical for rapid world-building.

As metaverse platforms evolve, they are shifting from local, device-dependent computing models towards harnessing the scale and capabilities of cloud computing and 5G networks. This approach, known as XR Cloud Platforms, extends the reach of Xtended Reality (XR) by offloading intensive rendering and processing tasks to external servers. Through this method, immersive graphics can be seamlessly streamed to lightweight client devices, enabling users to experience high-quality virtual environments without the burden of local hardware constraints.

NVIDIA's Omniverse is a multi-cloud platform that enables massive 3D simulations, photorealistic rendering, interactive AI models to collaboratively design and operate industrial metaverses at scale. BMW taps into Omniverse for automotive production leveraging AI.

Google's Immersive Stream for XR streams real-time sensor data to render rich 3D environments on the cloud for mobile augmented reality experiences. Similarly, Microsoft's Mesh builds shared immersive experiences for telepresence using Azure cloud compute.

These cloud XR platforms provide the scalable computing power, infrastructure, data connectivity, and tools required to operate expansive, persistent virtual worlds in the metaverse vision. Combined with digital twin capabilities, they enable real-time modelling and simulations that marry physical and virtual realities.

While amazing things are possible within today's fragmented metaverse pockets, we are still in the very early innings. Realising the full vision of an open, interoperable, and unified metaverse spanning worlds and platforms will require significant technological and collaborative progress. However, the core building blocks and ideals are taking shape across these diverse platforms.

Implications for the Future of the Metaverse

Metaverse platforms and environments hold significant implications for the future of technology, entertainment, and various industries. These platforms enable new opportunities for businesses to showcase products/services, engage with customers, and create immersive brand experiences. They also offer avenues for artists, designers, and creators to reach wider audiences and monetise their virtual creations.

In the realm of education, metaverse platforms can revolutionise learning by providing interactive and immersive experiences that transcend traditional classroom boundaries. Students can explore virtual historical sites, perform scientific experiments in simulated environments, and collaborate with peers from around the world.

However, challenges remain in realising the full potential of metaverse platforms. Interoperability between different platforms is crucial to creating a cohesive and connected metaverse, preventing fragmentation and ensuring seamless experiences across virtual worlds. Additionally, issues of privacy, security, and digital identity need to be addressed to maintain user trust and safety within the metaverse.

Conclusion

Metaverse platforms and environments are key building blocks in the development of the interconnected virtual world we envision as the metaverse. From virtual worlds ripe for exploration to user-generated content and virtual economies, these platforms offer endless opportunities for creativity, interaction, and immersion.

As the metaverse evolves, metaverse platforms will continue to evolve alongside it, enriching the virtual experiences of users and pushing the boundaries of what is possible. Collaboration between technology companies, content creators, and users will be vital in shaping a vibrant and interconnected metaverse that transcends physical limitations and sparks limitless imagination. By harnessing the potential of these platforms, we can build a metaverse that offers equal opportunities for all, enhances our lives, and redefines our understanding of human connectivity in the digital age.

Chapter 5
Key Components and Enabling Technologies of the Metaverse

The metaverse is a vivid and interconnected virtual reality that offers infinite possibilities for exploration, interaction, and creativity. As an ambitious technological convergence, it aims to blend the physical and digital worlds into seamless and persistent virtual experiences. Achieving this vision requires bringing together an array of advanced technologies and components that can collectively create a sense of presence, interoperability, and embodied realism. As the concept of the metaverse continues to capture the imagination of individuals worldwide, it is essential to delve deeper into its key components and enabling technologies. In this chapter, we will explore the foundational elements and cutting-edge technologies that make the metaverse a reality.

Some of the key technological pillars enabling the metaverse include:

1. Immersive User Experiences and Interfaces

Central to the metaverse is the ability to immerse users in virtual environments that stimulate their senses and blur the line between the physical and digital worlds. These environments can range from simulated replicas of real-world locations to entirely fictional realms. They are created using a combination of computer graphics, 3D modelling, and physics engines, allowing for realistic and dynamic experiences.

Technologies such as virtual reality (VR), augmented reality (AR), and mixed reality (MR) play crucial roles in creating these immersive experiences. VR allows users to be fully immersed in virtual worlds through headsets that provide a 360-degree view and tracking of their movements. AR overlays digital content onto the real world, enhancing real-life experiences with virtual elements. MR combines virtual and real-world elements, enabling users to interact with digital objects in their physical surroundings.

These immersive experiences are further enhanced by intuitive and user-friendly interfaces. Spatial computing, gesture recognition, and voice commands enable users to navigate and interact seamlessly within the metaverse.

XR, or Extended Reality, is an umbrella term that covers virtual reality (VR), augmented reality (AR), and mixed reality (MR). XR hardware like headsets, glasses, and contact lenses provide the sensory interfaces to fully immerse users in digital environments or blend them with the physical world.

High-fidelity, low-latency VR rigs using powerful graphics processing can create the illusion of being transported to entirely new virtual realms. Augmented reality smart glasses, on the other hand, overlay contextual information, holograms and digital assets atop the real world. Mixed reality combines the best of both - allowing seamless interaction between virtual and physical objects.

Advancements in display technologies, motion tracking, haptic feedback, and eye/gesture/voice-based controls are elevating XR as the centrepiece of metaverse experiences. Companies like Meta, Microsoft, Apple, and Sony are racing to deliver the next generation of consumer and enterprise XR devices.

2. Blockchain and Decentralisation

Blockchain technology, known for its transparent and secure nature, has emerged as a fundamental component of the metaverse. Decentralised platforms built on blockchain ensure ownership, transparency, and trust within the virtual ecosystem. This is accomplished through the use of smart contracts, which facilitate peer-to-peer transactions and secure ownership of digital assets.

The Ethereum blockchain, in particular, has gained prominence within the metaverse due to its ability to support smart contracts and the creation of non-fungible tokens (NFTs). Cryptocurrencies and Non-Fungible Tokens (NFTs) provide a means of exchange and ownership, allowing users to monetise their creations and establish a digital economy within the Metaverse.

NFTs, which can represent digital assets such as virtual land, art, or in-game items, enable creators and users to establish unique ownership and monetisation opportunities within the metaverse.

This unlocks the potential for metaverse participants to build thriving digital economies, where users can buy, sell, and trade virtual real estate, wearables, art, and experiences. Decentralised finance (DeFi) protocols can further enable frictionless payments, lending, and investment in these virtual realms.

Beyond simple ownership, smart contracts can also encode complex rights, royalties, and programmable behaviours into digital assets. This lays the foundation for a creator economy where users are empowered to build, monetise, and govern their own virtual creations.

3. Interoperability and Standards

The metaverse comprises a multitude of interconnected platforms and virtual worlds. Interoperability and standards play a critical role in enabling seamless transfer of assets, avatars, and experiences between different environments.

Interoperability standards such as the Open Metaverse Interoperability Group (OMG) and the Virtual Reality and Augmented Reality Association (VRARA) are working towards establishing common protocols and frameworks for the metaverse. These efforts aim to create a unified metaverse experience, allowing users to seamlessly navigate and interact across various platforms.

Standards for avatars, assets, and other elements of the metaverse are also crucial for enabling interoperability. The use of open formats, such as glTF and USDZ, ensures that assets can be easily shared and used across different metaverse platforms.

4. Artificial Intelligence (AI) and Machine Learning (ML)

AI and ML technologies are fundamental in creating dynamic and responsive metaverse environments. These technologies enable lifelike characters and NPCs (non-player characters) that interact with users, adapting and evolving based on user behaviour and preferences.

Natural Language Processing (NLP) and computer vision techniques enable realistic and engaging conversations with virtual characters, enhancing the interactive experiences within the metaverse. AI-powered tools also assist in content creation, providing automated algorithms for generating landscapes, objects, and virtual characters.

5. Cloud Computing and Edge Computing

Cloud computing and edge computing are essential technologies that provide the necessary computing power and storage capabilities for the vast and complex metaverse.

Cloud computing involves storing and managing large amounts of data in centralised servers, which helps ensure smooth user experiences and collaboration within the metaverse. It allows users to access and interact with virtual worlds without worrying about the technical details of where the data is stored.

Edge computing, on the other hand, brings computing power closer to the user, reducing delays and enabling instant interactions in resource-intensive metaverse experiences. This means that processing data closer to where it is needed helps in providing faster and more responsive virtual experiences for users.

In simple terms, cloud computing handles the overall storage and management of data for the metaverse, while edge computing focuses on delivering quick responses and interactions within these virtual environments by processing data closer to the users. Together, they ensure that users can navigate and interact with the metaverse smoothly and in real-time.

6. Internet of Things (IoT)

The Internet of Things (IoT) is a crucial technology that helps connect the physical and virtual worlds within the metaverse. IoT devices, such as sensors, wearables, and smart objects, play an important role by providing real-time data that enhances the virtual environment and user experiences.

For example, imagine you are exploring a virtual world within the metaverse that represents a forest. IoT sensors placed in the real-world forest can capture information like weather conditions, temperature, and movement of animals. This real-world data can then be integrated into the metaverse, making the virtual forest more dynamic and realistic.

Additionally, IoT devices can enable physical interactions within the metaverse by controlling smart objects and appliances in the real world. For instance, you could use an IoT device to turn on the lights in your actual house while you are immersed in a virtual home within the metaverse.

In simpler terms, IoT devices gather real-world data and bring it into the virtual world of the metaverse, making it more immersive and authentic. They also allow users to control real-world objects through the virtual environment, enhancing the connection between the physical and digital realms.

7. Avatars and Identity

Avatars are like digital versions of users within the Metaverse. They allow people to explore and interact within virtual environments, giving them a sense of presence and control. Avatars have become more advanced thanks to improvements in customisation, motion capture, and animation technologies. This means that users can create unique and realistic digital personas, making the Metaverse feel more immersive.

Advancements in technology have made it possible for avatars to mimic users' movements, facial expressions, and even their voice. This is done through real-time motion capture and facial tracking. Avatars can now look and behave like the people controlling them. There are even techniques, like generative adversarial networks, to create highly realistic digital human avatars.

Additionally, avatars can engage in conversations and interact meaningfully in the Metaverse. This is made possible by conversational AI, machine learning, and knowledge graphs. Virtual assistants, digital companions, and non-player characters can populate these virtual worlds, making them more lively and responsive.

In simpler terms, avatars are the digital representations of users in the Metaverse. They can look and act like real people, thanks to advanced technologies. Avatars can mirror users' movements and expressions, and they can even have conversations with other characters in the virtual world. All of this makes the Metaverse feel more realistic and engaging.

8. Spatial Computing

Spatial computing is an important technology that helps create immersive experiences in the Metaverse. It involves digitally modelling and understanding the 3D physical world in real-time. Spatial computing uses technologies like computer vision and depth sensing to allow the Metaverse to understand and interact with the real world. These technologies enable virtual objects to be integrated into real-world spaces and enable interactions based on the user's physical presence and movements.

For example, spatial computing enables augmented reality experiences in the Metaverse. It combines digital elements with the physical environment to create interactive and immersive experiences. This is achieved using cameras, depth sensors, LIDAR scanners, and computer vision algorithms to accurately understand and reconstruct environments.

Spatial computing is essential for seamlessly blending digital and physical elements within the Metaverse. It can track surfaces, objects, and even human body movements, creating an interactive and realistic virtual world.

One of the applications of spatial computing is the creation of digital twins. These are virtual replicas of real-world entities, systems, or processes. Digital twins can be used to mirror physical assets, cities, or supply chains. They allow for remote collaboration, simulation, and predictive maintenance, enhancing efficiency and productivity within the Metaverse.

In simpler terms, spatial computing is the technology that helps the Metaverse understand and interact with the physical world. It allows virtual content to be integrated into real-world spaces and enables virtual experiences that feel realistic and immersive. Spatial computing also enables the creation of digital replicas of the real world, which can be used for various purposes like remote collaboration and simulation.

Exploring different applications in the Metavese world with different headsets and accessories (Pic credit – Metaverse911)

Conclusion

The metaverse is built on a foundation of key components and enabling technologies that bring the virtual world to life. Immersive experiences, blockchain and decentralisation, interoperability, AI and

ML, cloud and edge computing, and the IoT all play vital roles in creating a seamless and captivating metaverse environment.

As these technologies continue to advance, grow, and interconnect, the possibilities of the metaverse will only expand. The metaverse has the potential to revolutionise how we interact, work, learn, and entertain ourselves. It opens up new avenues for creativity, collaboration, and economic opportunities, redefining the way we perceive and engage with the world around us.

Of course, realising the grand vision will require overcoming significant technical and societal challenges. But the pieces are coming together to enable a more seamless convergence of our physical and digital existences.

Chapter 6
Metaverse and Virtual Economies
Cryptocurrencies, NFTs, and Ownership

The Metaverse, a virtual reality space where users can interact and immerse themselves in a vast digital world, has become highly intriguing due to its potential impact on various industries. As the metaverse vision unfolds, one of its most transformative aspects will be the rise of thriving digital economies powered by cryptocurrencies, NFTs, and new models of virtual asset ownership. These Web3 technologies will enable participants to freely create, buy, sell, and trade a vast array of digital goods and experiences.

At the heart of the metaverse's economic potential lies the concept of digital scarcity and verifiable ownership. Unlike traditional digital goods that can be endlessly replicated, blockchain technology allows the creation of unique, provably scarce digital assets. This paves the way for digital collectibles, virtual land parcels, avatar wearables, and other one-of-a-kind virtual items to hold genuine value.

The Rise of NFTs

NFTs, or non-fungible tokens, have become the leading method for representing and trading unique digital assets. They are transforming how we think about ownership, particularly in the Metaverse. Unlike cryptocurrencies, which are interchangeable (one Bitcoin is the same as another), NFTs represent one-of-a-kind digital items, such as virtual real estate, digital art, or even virtual fashion. NFTs are becoming increasingly popular because they enable users to verify ownership of a specific digital item in ways that were not possible before.

To better understand NFTs, think of them as special digital certificates stored on a blockchain. These certificates confirm that you own a particular digital item, such as a piece of digital art or an in-game item. Unlike physical goods, which can be copied, NFTs cannot be replicated, ensuring the digital asset remains rare and valuable—much like owning a limited edition of a famous painting.

After understanding that NFTs are unique, you might wonder how it's possible to have multiple copies of the same artwork or collectible, such as a signed autograph by Amitabh Bachchan, a painting by Salman Khan, clips from Lionel Messi's iconic goals or matches, or exclusive digital wearables by Shawn Mendes. While these items may appear identical, the uniqueness of NFTs lies in the ownership recorded on the blockchain. Each NFT acts as a digital certificate of ownership, distinguishing it from other copies, even if they look the same. The blockchain ensures that each NFT carries a unique history of ownership, making it clear who owns the original version of the item.

The key difference lies in ownership and verification. For example, consider two digital copies of the Mona Lisa—one owned by you and another owned by your friend Kashmira. While the image may look identical, the NFT associated with each one certifies a unique digital proof of ownership. The blockchain tracks who owns each copy and records its transaction history, ensuring that the original, verified version is traceable.

This is what makes the Mona Lisa in NFT form unique. It's not about the visual copy, but about blockchain-based ownership that cannot be faked, duplicated, or transferred without a record. The NFT serves as the official certificate of ownership, providing irrefutable proof of who truly owns the item—unlike traditional copies, which may look the same but lack verified ownership.

Thus, while the visual representation of the Mona Lisa may be identical in both copies, the NFT associated with each one has a unique identity based on characteristics like timestamps, owner information, and transaction history. The blockchain ensures that the original, verified version remains traceable. In this way, NFTs offer a unique, digital certificate of ownership that cannot be copied or duplicated. It's not about the picture itself but the proof of who owns the official version—much like a signed book or a limited-edition print, but secured by blockchain technology.

By tokenising virtual goods as NFTs, the Metaverse unlocks a new frontier of digital ownership. Users can possess, control, and extract value from their virtual creations and acquisitions. NFTs enable portability—users can freely move, trade, or monetise their virtual items across different metaverse environments, bypassing the limitations of proprietary platforms.

Tokenising virtual goods as NFTs refers to the process of turning something digital into a unique, blockchain-backed token. If you have a virtual fashion item or digital art, it is "tokenised" by associating it with an NFT. This process gives the item a unique identity that can be traded, sold, or collected, much like physical items with certificates of authenticity. Tokenising a digital item essentially creates a verified ownership certificate for that content, ensuring it cannot be replicated, and your ownership of it is secure.

Here's how the process works, broken down into simple steps:

1. **Choose the Digital Item**: Select the digital asset you want to turn into an NFT, such as digital art, music, videos, virtual land, or in-game items.

2. **Create the NFT**: Upload the item to an NFT-supporting platform like OpenSea or Rarible. The platform links the item with a blockchain, creating a unique digital token for it.

3. **Minting the NFT**: Minting is the process of turning the digital item into a unique token on the blockchain. This token proves ownership and ensures authenticity, making it impossible to duplicate.

4. **Assign Ownership**: The NFT is assigned to your digital wallet, where it's stored, and you become the official owner of the token—just like holding a physical item in your possession.

5. **Buying and Selling the NFT**: Once you own the NFT, you can keep it, sell it, or trade it on an NFT marketplace.

Blockchain keeps track of the transactions, ensuring clear and secure ownership.

Additionally, NFTs can carry smart contracts that automatically handle tasks like managing rights, distributing royalties, and executing programmed actions. For example, owning an NFT for a virtual fashion item might grant you the right to wear it across various metaverse platforms and earn a share of the proceeds whenever it's resold. This provides creators with a way to continue earning from their work long after the initial sale, without intermediaries.

In essence, tokenising digital items transforms them into unique, valuable assets in the digital world, providing new opportunities for creators and collectors alike.

Expanding Beyond Digital Art

There is more to NFTs than just digital art. While NFTs are commonly associated with collectibles like virtual art, they are also being utilised for virtual real estate, in-game assets, and even virtual fashion. For instance, owning virtual land in the Metaverse or acquiring a special in-game item can hold significant value, sometimes even surpassing the worth of digital art. In these scenarios, NFTs offer a way to authenticate ownership of virtual assets that serve a practical function within digital environments. These types of NFTs go beyond simple representation, giving users a tangible stake in virtual worlds and making the concept of ownership more dynamic and multifaceted.

Cryptocurrencies in the Metaverse

Cryptocurrencies have become a fundamental component of the Metaverse, facilitating various economic transactions within virtual worlds. Virtual currencies, such as Bitcoin, Ethereum, and other digital tokens, enable users to buy and sell virtual assets seamlessly. Being decentralised and blockchain-based, these digital currencies bring security, transparency, and ownership verification to virtual transactions that traditional fiat currencies cannot provide. Consequently, virtual economies with their thriving marketplaces have emerged, allowing users to trade digital assets. Moreover, cryptocurrencies serve as the native medium of exchange underpinning these burgeoning metaverse economies. Stablecoins, governance tokens, and other blockchain-based digital currencies facilitate frictionless peer-to-peer transactions, micro-payments, and new monetisation models within virtual worlds.

Unlike traditional fiat-based in-game currencies or credits, crypto assets can be freely exchanged, withdrawn, and used outside the confines of any single metaverse platform. This interoperability is crucial, as it allows value accrued in one virtual environment to be portable and usable in others.

Decentralised finance (DeFi) protocols built on blockchains can also integrate directly with metaverse economies. This enables novel financial services like lending, borrowing, and yield farming of virtual assets and resources. Users can leverage their digital holdings to access liquidity, generate yield, or even speculate on the future value of virtual real estate and items.

Understanding the Difference Between NFTs and Cryptocurrencies

Both NFTs (Non-Fungible Tokens) and cryptocurrencies like Bitcoin or Ethereum use blockchain technology, but they serve different purposes.

- **Cryptocurrencies** are digital currencies that are interchangeable. As an example, one Bitcoin holds the same value as another, functioning as both a medium for transactions and a store of wealth, just like regular currency.

- **NFTs**, however, are unique tokens representing ownership of a specific digital item. In contrast to cryptocurrencies, NFTs are unique and cannot be traded on a one-to-one basis. They are frequently used to establish ownership of digital assets like art, virtual land, or collectibles.

In simple terms, cryptocurrencies are like digital money, while NFTs are like certificates of ownership for digital items. Understanding this difference helps explain their roles in the Metaverse and beyond.

Ownership in the Metaverse

The concept of ownership in the Metaverse has undergone a significant transformation. In the past, ownership was mainly associated with physical assets and properties. However, with the emergence of the Metaverse, ownership now extends to virtual assets as well. The idea of "digital scarcity" – meaning that virtual items can be made rare or limited, just like physical objects – has led to the creation of virtual assets that hold real-world value. Unlike digital files that can be easily copied, blockchain technology ensures these virtual assets are unique and cannot be replicated, making them scarce. This blurring of boundaries between physical and digital realms has been further enhanced by blockchain, which provides indisputable proof of ownership and prevents fraudulent transactions. This empowerment enables users to have full control over their virtual assets, allowing them to transfer, sell, or lend them to others within the Metaverse.

Beyond trading, the Metaverse also introduces new models for digital content creation and monetisation. By combining NFTs, cryptocurrency, and decentralised autonomous organisations (DAOs), creators can directly earn from, retain ownership of, and govern the virtual experiences they create. For instance, a 3D fashion designer can turn their virtual garment designs into NFTs, sell them directly to users, and receive royalties each time the NFT is resold - all without the need for an intermediary platform that takes a large cut. Additionally, creators in the Metaverse can form DAOs to collectively own, manage, and profit from shared virtual worlds and experiences.

The Implications

The integration of cryptocurrencies, NFTs, and ownership within the Metaverse has far-reaching implications across various industries. Gaming, for instance, has been greatly influenced by these developments. Virtual economies have introduced a new dimension to gaming, creating opportunities for in-game purchases, virtual property investments, and digital asset trading. Additionally, the entertainment industry has begun exploring the possibilities of virtual concerts, live events, and immersive experiences. The utilisation of cryptocurrencies and NFTs provides a means to reward content creators directly and maintain the integrity of their work. Similarly, the educational and healthcare sectors are harnessing the potential of the Metaverse to develop immersive learning experiences and telemedicine applications.

Practical Applications of NFTs in the Metaverse

1. Digital Collectibles and Art

NFTs have revolutionised the art world, providing artists with a new medium to showcase and monetise their work. Platforms such as **OpenSea** and **Foundation** allow creators to tokenise digital art, offering collectors unique pieces that are verifiably scarce. Digital art in the form of NFTs not only brings monetary value to creators but also ensures ownership rights and provenance, enabling artists to earn royalties from secondary sales.

Example: Beeple, a digital artist, sold his digital artwork "EVERYDAYS: THE FIRST 5000 DAYS" for $69 million, exemplifying how NFTs (non-fungible tokens) are reshaping the value of digital art and making it a lucrative sector within the metaverse.

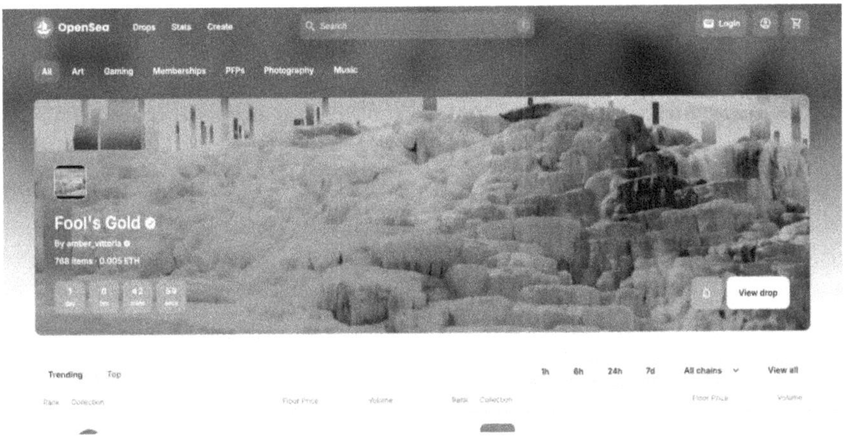

Opensea Marketplace for NFTs

2. Virtual Real Estate

Virtual real estate in platforms like **Decentraland** and **The Sandbox** exemplifies the application of NFTs in representing ownership of digital land. Users can buy, sell, and develop parcels of land, with ownership secured on the blockchain. These virtual plots can be used for various purposes, such as building virtual homes, hosting events, or creating digital businesses.

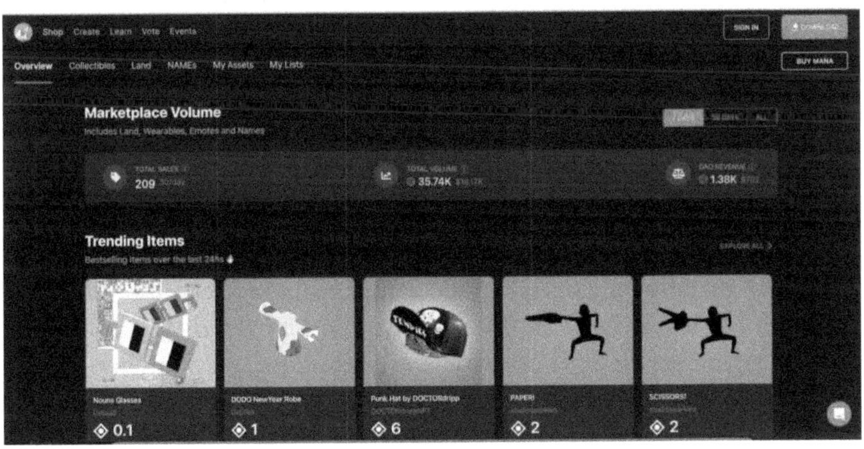

Decentraland Marketplace for Virtual Land

3. Gaming and In-Game Assets

Games like **Axie Infinity** and **The Sandbox** utilise NFTs to provide players with true ownership of their in-game items. Players can trade these items on secondary markets, monetising their gaming efforts. This ownership model enhances player engagement by allowing users to earn real-world value from virtual assets.

4. Fashion and Virtual Wearables

NFTs are also revolutionising the fashion industry within the metaverse. Digital fashion items, tokenised as NFTs, enable users to customise their avatars with unique wearables. Platforms like **The Fabricant** and **RTFKT Studios** collaborate with fashion brands to create virtual clothing, merging the physical and digital fashion worlds.

5. Music and Entertainment

Musicians are leveraging NFTs to tokenise their work, offering exclusive tracks, albums, and experiences directly to fans. This model empowers artists by decentralising distribution and providing direct revenue streams. NFTs also enable unique fan interactions, such as virtual concert access and personalised content.

6. Sports Collectibles and Memorabilia

Sports organisations are increasingly adopting NFTs to create digital collectibles, such as trading cards and highlight reels. **NBA Top Shot** is a prominent example, where fans can buy, sell, and trade officially licensed NBA moments. This model extends the traditional sports memorabilia market into the digital realm, offering verifiable ownership and scarcity.

Challenges and Future Prospects

As excitement and innovation grow around the Metaverse and its virtual economies, it's crucial to recognise and tackle the challenges that come with this shift. Privacy and security concerns, interoperability issues, legal and ethical considerations, and the scalability and user-friendliness of blockchain technology all need careful attention to ensure responsible development and widespread use of the Metaverse.

Transitioning to a user-owned metaverse economy also faces hurdles like regulatory uncertainty regarding the legal status of NFTs, intellectual property issues, and worries about the environmental impact of blockchain networks. Despite these challenges, the core principles of digital scarcity, decentralised ownership, and self-sovereign value creation continue to drive innovation and change in the digital space. The future of the Metaverse looks promising, with the potential to revolutionise how we live, work, and interact in a digitised world.

Conclusion

The integration of cryptocurrencies, NFTs, and ownership within the Metaverse has opened up new possibilities in virtual economies. The use of cryptocurrencies facilitates seamless transactions, while the advent of NFTs brings authenticity and uniqueness to digital assets. Ownership in the Metaverse enables users to exercise control over their virtual possessions, blurring the line between the physical and digital realms. As the Metaverse continues to evolve, the potential for economic growth, immersive experiences, and creative expression becomes even more apparent. With proper considerations for privacy, security, and ethical frameworks, the future of the Metaverse holds vast opportunities for innovation and connectivity.

Chapter 7
Immersive User Experiences and Interfaces in the Metaverse

In the ever-expanding landscape of the Metaverse, the concept of immersive user experiences and interfaces holds paramount importance. As technology progresses, the ability to engage users in rich, and interactive environments becomes increasingly vital. In this chapter, we delve into the immersive user experiences and interfaces that define the Metaverse and explore their implications for users, developers, and the broader digital ecosystem.

At the core of the metaverse vision lies the promise of profoundly immersive and embodied digital experiences that seamlessly blend with our physical reality. Creating this sense of presence involves moving beyond the flat, two-dimensional interfaces that currently dominate our digital interactions. Immersive user experiences in the Metaverse encompass a wide range of elements, from virtual reality (VR) and augmented reality (AR) to mixed reality (MR) environments. These experiences aim to transport users into virtual worlds where they can interact with digital content and other users in a seamless and immersive manner. Through advanced technologies such as spatial computing, haptic feedback, and photorealistic graphics, users can feel fully immersed in their virtual surroundings, blurring the lines between the physical and digital realms.

The metaverse demands intuitive, multi-modal interfaces that can effectively transport users into vivid virtual worlds while also enhancing how we perceive and navigate the real world around us. This new era of computing will leverage a range of innovative technologies and interaction paradigms to deliver truly immersive experiences.

Lifelike Virtual Environments

To feel truly present, users need to be enveloped in richly detailed, photorealistic virtual environments that stimulate all the human senses. At the visual level, advancements in real-time ray tracing, volumetric capture, and physically-based rendering are already enabling breathtakingly lifelike digital worlds. Game engines like Unreal 5 showcase stunning simulated environments with cinematic fidelity, imbued with accurate light physics, pixel-perfect geometry, and dynamic global illumination. Features like MetaHuman Creator help generate incredibly realistic digital humans.

On the audio front, spatial and ambisonic sound design creates incredibly immersive 3D soundscapes that replicate acoustics and directional audio cues. Haptic wearables can simulate physical sensations of touch, texture, and force feedback corresponding to virtual object interactions.

From reactive weather systems and foliage to visceral sound effects and tangible surfaces, the metaverse's virtual realms aim to provide a level of simulated realism that credibly tricks human perception.

Embodied Interfaces

One of the key aspects of immersive user experiences in the Metaverse is the role of interfaces. Beyond recreating physical environments, the metaverse depends on naturalistic and intuitive ways for users to navigate and interact in these virtual spaces as embodied avatars. Interfaces serve as the gateway for users to interact with virtual environments, enabling them to navigate, manipulate objects, and communicate with others. Traditional interfaces, such as keyboards, mice, and touch screens, are being augmented and replaced by more intuitive and immersive interfaces, including gesture recognition, voice commands, and brain-computer interfaces (BCIs). These interfaces offer new ways for users to interact with digital content, enhancing the overall immersion and usability of the Metaverse.

Computer vision, motion capture, eye tracking, and gesture recognition empower users to control digital objects and experiences using natural hand and body gestures. Embedded sensors detect limb positions for intuitively puppet-mastering avatars. Advanced voice interfaces allow spoken commands to manipulate virtual assets.

Brain-computer interfaces that translate neural activity into control inputs could eventually replace handheld controllers entirely, enabling users to navigate simply through thoughts and muscle twitches. As we blend physical and digital realms, our human behaviours and muscle memory become the interfaces.

Augmented Reality Interfaces

On the augmented reality side, intuitive AR interfaces aim to make the digital seamlessly meld with the physical environment in meaningful ways. AR visualisations, graphics, and data overlays need to dynamically map and adapt to surrounding spaces and surfaces.

Gesture tracking and gaze detection let users intuitively summon and control these virtual AR elements using their hands and eyesight as the input. Voice commands further enhance hands-free operation. Spatial audio provides auditory cues synchronised with digital content positions.

The ultimate AR interface envisions virtual control and contextual visualisations intuitively floating within our physical spaces. We'd simply reach out and touch holograms, or engage in physical collaborations enhanced by projected digital information and tools.

Wearable Computing

For these seamless interface paradigms to work, wearable devices and access points are crucial. VR headsets with hand tracking and real-time eye tracking serve as the primary conduit into fully virtual environments. AR capabilities embedded into smart glasses overlay digital elements within real-world contexts.

Other wearables like haptic gloves, motion trackers, and even augmented reality contact lenses further immerse users. As connectivity and processing power improve, today's bulky headsets could eventually miniaturise into lightweight frames blending digital and physical realms nearly indistinguishably.

Beyond dedicated wearables, mobile devices, consumer electronics, and even our living spaces themselves could all become interactive access points bridging the real and virtual worlds.

To optimise for presence and embodiment, the metaverse experience aims to fade interfaces into invisibility, allowing users to directly manipulate virtual objects as naturally as physical ones. Inputs like voice, body movements, eye tracking, and even neural signals let us intuitively cross between realities - lowering adoption friction and cognitive load.

Another important consideration in immersive user experiences is accessibility. As the Metaverse becomes more mainstream, ensuring that all users, regardless of their abilities, can participate and engage with virtual environments is essential. Designing inclusive interfaces that accommodate diverse needs and preferences is crucial for creating a truly immersive and accessible Metaverse. This includes considerations such as providing alternative input methods, customizable interfaces, and support for assistive technologies.

Furthermore, the design of immersive user experiences and interfaces in the Metaverse is heavily influenced by human factors and cognitive psychology. Understanding how users perceive, process, and interact with digital content is essential for creating compelling and engaging experiences. Factors such as attention, memory, and perception play a significant role in shaping user interactions and interface design decisions. By applying principles from cognitive science and human-computer interaction (HCI), developers can create interfaces that are intuitive, efficient, and enjoyable to use.

In addition to enhancing user experiences, immersive interfaces in the Metaverse also offer new opportunities for content creation and expression. With tools such as virtual reality sculpting, 3D modelling, and spatial design, users can unleash their creativity and bring their ideas to life in virtual space. Whether designing virtual environments, creating digital artwork, or building interactive experiences, the Metaverse provides a canvas for limitless creativity and expression.

Experiencing Metaverse in a Metaverse Experience Center at Metaverse911 Studio based in India.

Mixed Reality Interfaces

Bridging the gap between fully virtual and augmented reality experiences, mixed reality (MR) interfaces blend physical and digital in a hybrid mode. With MR, users can intuitively interact with and manipulate virtual 3D objects anchored within their real-world surroundings.

MR experiences leverage many of the same technologies as VR and AR, such as environment mapping, spatial tracking, and gesture recognition. However, the interfaces aim to provide a true "spatial computing" experience where digital and physical elements seamlessly coexist.

For example, MR interfaces may allow users to summon holographic 3D models into their workspace that can be resized, repositioned, or disassembled using natural hand motions. Alternatively, virtual instructional guides or collaborative annotation tools could be overlaid onto real objects to provide immersive training or remote assistance.

As MR headsets like the Microsoft HoloLens evolve, advanced computer vision and machine learning will enable increasingly contextual experiences. The headsets can understand the semantics of a scene to have virtual elements intelligently adapt based on the existing physical geometry and surfaces.

Moreover, immersive user experiences and interfaces have profound implications for various industries and applications within the Metaverse. In fields such as gaming, entertainment, education, and virtual events, immersive interfaces play a central role in delivering engaging and memorable experiences to users. From immersive storytelling and virtual concerts to interactive learning environments and collaborative workspaces, the Metaverse offers a wealth of possibilities for innovation and exploration.

Ultimately, MR's interfaces aspire to dissolve the boundaries between digital and physical realms into a true "spatial operating system." Users simply use direct hand interactions and voice commands to summon and manipulate virtual assets that are anchored persistently in their real environments.

The end goal is to seamlessly blend the interfaces until they become invisible - allowing users to freely navigate the blurring boundaries between digital and physical realms while retaining a sense of natural embodied presence. As computational power increases and XR interfaces miniaturise, the command prompts and controllers that have long dominated computing may ultimately give way to more naturalistic, multi-modal ways of experiencing the metaverse.

Pillow is a unique mixed reality app for the Meta Quest headset, specifically designed for use while lying down. It offers four interactive experiences that help users relax and unwind, transforming the ceiling into various immersive environments.|

Chapter 8
Social and Economic Implications of the Metaverse
Multiplayer Gaming, Entertainment, and Events

As the metaverse takes shape, it promises to revolutionise how we play, socialise, and experience entertainment. The combination of immersive virtual environments, embodied avatars, and converging digital economies opens up vast new possibilities in areas like multiplayer gaming, live events, and virtual concerts.

At its core, the metaverse facilitates profoundly social virtual experiences by providing richly interactive 3D spaces for people to co-exist, regardless of physical proximity. These are not solitary virtual worlds, but rather massively multiplayer persistent realms where users represented by avatars can freely explore, interact, collaborate, and forge communities.

Gaming and the Metaverse

Video games like Fortnite, Roblox, and Minecraft are at the forefront of developing what's known as the "metaverse." This term refers to interconnected virtual worlds where users can engage in a variety of activities, including gaming, socialising, and creative expression.

Within these gaming environments, players not only participate in gameplay but also have the opportunity to interact socially, create their own content, and attend virtual events such as concerts. These features represent early manifestations of the metaverse concept, demonstrating its potential for multifaceted experiences beyond mere gaming.

As the metaverse continues to evolve, gaming will serve as a foundational element within these expansive virtual environments. Games will become increasingly immersive and realistic, serving as persistent spaces for leisure activities, social gatherings, and cultural events.

Moreover, the principles and dynamics inherent to gaming—such as interactivity, avatar embodiment, and user-generated content—will significantly influence the design and cultural norms of the emerging metaverse. These elements play a crucial role in shaping the user experience and community dynamics within virtual environments.

Virtual Events and Shared Experiences

Live events are another core pillar of metaverse experiences that are rapidly evolving. Concerts, conferences, comedy shows, and other performances are already being hosted virtually using VR/AR/Mixed-reality platforms.

These virtualised events enable new possibilities – a sense of shared presence without physical constraints of venue size or location. Avatars allow participants to embody unique personas and self-expression. There are new creative canvases for artists and organisers to stage mind-bending experiences transcending physical limits.

Platforms like Horizon Venues by Meta host immersive VR concerts and comedy shows attended by avatar audiences. Users can congregate in expansive virtual auditoriums, interact with fan-merchandise stores and freely roam to find optimal vantage points for these live performances.

Facebook Horizon worlds

Alternatively, events can transcend purely virtual modes through mixed reality integrations. Artists can appear as photorealistic holograms beamed into physical spaces, or real-world fans could join VR audiences using AR overlays. Hybrid models blend the best of physical and virtual realms for events.

Beyond entertainment, the same virtual events paradigm could replicate conventions, trade shows, or professional conferences, enabling connection between remote attendees in shared virtual lobbies, auditoriums and networking areas.

Social Platforms and Digital Communities

More generally, shared immersive experiences enabled by the metaverse principle can facilitate entirely new modes of digital socialising and identity expression. Much like social media and messaging apps revolutionised communication, metaverse platforms aim to pioneer virtual social networks transcending flat 2D planes.

Instead of static profiles on feeds, users will interact as fully embodied 3D avatars in communal virtual hangouts and spaces. Shared experiences and commentary within virtual "third spaces" could become as prevalent as texting and posting in today's digital landscapes.

Early glimpses of this behaviour already manifest in virtual social worlds like VR Chat or Alt-SpaceVR. People's digital egos and avatars become immersive personas allowing greater creative self-expression. Complex identities and status hierarchies emerge in these vibrant virtual realms hosting meetups, games, performances and events.

This virtualisation of how humans congregate could extend beyond just shared social platforms into thriving digital communities, economies and civilizations wholly self-organising and governing within the metaverse's realm. Much as how the internet birthed innovative business and cultural models, the metaverse has equal transformative potential to reshape societal interactions, not just entertain or socialise.

Economic Implications

The rise of immersive virtual experiences and economies in the metaverse will heavily rely on digital assets, currencies, micropayments, and ownership mechanisms linked to blockchain technology and cryptographic tokens.

These digital assets, which can include everything from virtual goods to wearable items for avatars, are not just for cosmetic purposes—they also introduce new ways for people to participate in and make money from virtual environments.

For example, creators, performers, and influencers can earn income by selling virtual goods directly or hosting events where attendees pay with cryptocurrency. Additionally, in-game items can now be truly owned and traded as Non-Fungible Tokens (NFTs) between players and collectors.

Furthermore, people who contribute value to virtual worlds—such as by designing structures or moderating communities—could receive compensation in the form of governance tokens, which represent a stake in decision-making processes within these virtual communities.

One of the most exciting aspects of these digital assets is their interoperability, meaning they can be used across different virtual worlds and experiences. This means that assets earned or purchased in one game or realm can retain their value and usefulness as users explore various parts of the expansive metaverse.

Participation in the metaverse transforms from merely consuming content to actively contributing and having a stake in the virtual world. Through token-based incentive systems, individuals are incentivised to engage with the virtual environment, thereby sharing in its value and ownership.

These incentive structures, powered by tokens, encourage people to participate more actively while ensuring that the benefits are distributed among the community members. This shift empowers users to become stakeholders in the virtual realm, rather than passive consumers.

The economic and cultural implications of integrating multiplayer games, social networks, digital ownership, and the convergence of real-world and virtual experiences within shared virtual realms are profound. While still in its early stages, we can already see the potential of these virtual domains through the innovative efforts of trailblazers pushing the boundaries of what's possible.

How society embraces and shapes these virtual spaces will be a defining challenge for future generations. The decisions made today regarding the development and governance of the metaverse will have long-lasting effects on our economic, social, and cultural landscapes.

Chapter 9
Avatars and Identity in the Metaverse

In the metaverse, our digital selves manifest as fully embodied 3D avatars that serve as our vehicles for exploration, self-expression, and interaction across immersive virtual experiences. More than just static profile pictures, metaverse avatars aim to become lifelike embodiments of our identities, personas, and very presence within these interconnected realms.

As we transition from observing content on flat 2D screens to inhabiting richly spatial virtual worlds, avatars emerge as powerful tools for presence and representation. They act as our proxies in the metaverse - enabling us to vividly experience these simulated environments while also projecting facets of our real identities into digital form.

Meta Avatars (Picture credit - Meta)

At their core, metaverse avatars need to be highly customizable digital mannequins that users can imbue with personal flair, from facial features and body types down to clothing, accessories, and personality traits. Contemporary games and social VR platforms already showcase extensive avatar editors that empower creativity.

However, the metaverse demands avatar systems that transcend gaming caricatures into digital humans indistinguishable from reality itself. Extraordinary advancements in fields like 3D graphics, motion capture, facial animation, and simulation are paving the way for stunningly realistic and lifelike digital avatars that can credibly encapsulate our identities.

Photorealistic Digital Humans

At the forefront of creating incredibly realistic avatars is Epic Games' MetaHuman technology. This technology, powered by advanced machine learning and motion capture techniques, can generate digital humans with an unprecedented level of realism. These avatars feature intricate details such as individual hair strands, lifelike skin textures with visible pores, realistic teeth, and natural eye movements.

Other companies, like Faceware, focus on capturing the subtle nuances of facial expressions and emotions using motion capture sensors. This allows for the creation of animated avatars in the metaverse that can convey a wide range of human communication cues, both verbal and non-verbal.

As technology continues to advance, users will have the ability to create hyper-realistic avatars that closely resemble their real-world selves. Achieving this level of realism is crucial for users to feel a strong sense of presence in the virtual world.

However, not everyone may prefer photorealistic avatars. Some users may opt for stylised fantasy avatars with artistic or idealised features that reflect their imagination and aspirations. These diverse representation options allow users to express themselves in unique ways within the metaverse.

Stylised Avatar Personalisation

While realistic representations may be ideal for collaborative and professional settings in the metaverse, consumers are likely to embrace rich stylised avatar personalisation for entertainment, games, online hangouts and self-expression.

Platforms like Decentraland and Cryptovoxels let users construct creative voxel-based avatars and environments from the ground up. Roblox empowers near-endless avatar customisation and personalisation options - especially popular among young users.

As the metaverse evolves, users could transform their avatars through increasingly sophisticated customisation mechanics spanning attire, accessories, facial features, body shapes, materials, colours, and even whimsical, fantastical creature designs. Vibrant digital fashion and avatar aesthetic personalisation could manifest as major lifestyle and identity pillars.

In-depth avatar editing tools and character creators will be crucial for users to craft digital personas matching their imagination, creativity, and self-image. Rather than standardised templates, the metaverse should empower nuanced self-identity formation and exploration across a spectrum of realism and imagination. Having detailed editing tools for avatars will be important so users can create characters that match their imagination and personality. Instead of having to pick from preset options, people should be able to create avatars that truly represent who they are or who they want to be.

Moreover, these avatars should persist as persistent identities representing users not just across virtual worlds and platforms, but also dynamically evolving alongside users' changing self-perceptions and identity growth over time. To be more specific, these avatars shouldn't just be limited to one platform or world. They should stick with users wherever they go in the metaverse, growing and changing along with them as they discover new things about themselves and how they want to be seen online.

Avatar Progression and Inheritability

Just as we experience maturation through different phases of our human identities across the real world, metaverse avatars should be designed for progression and heirloom ability across experiences. Similar to humans, metaverse avatars should also evolve as they move through various experiences. An avatar used as a youthful persona could cosmetically evolve into a mature professional digital identity for work environments and formal gatherings. Starting off with a young and playful appearance, these avatars have the flexibility to transform into a more mature and professional look, tailored for work-related tasks or formal occasions.

Avatars could serve as persistent, inheritable representations that can be seamlessly transported along with digital inventories and wearables across multiple virtual realms and platforms. Advanced machine learning models could continuously analyse users' actual appearance, voice, speech patterns, behaviours and more - to keep dynamic avatars synchronised and constantly updated with evolving real-world counterparts.

Furthermore, avatars could branch out into different versions tailored for specific situations, such as office settings, casual hangouts, or fantasy role-playing scenarios. These variations would be compatible across different virtual environments, ensuring users' identities remain consistent across diverse online spaces.

Identity and Reputation Systems

As user identity in the metaverse blends our real-world and digital selves, robust authentication systems will become crucial for linking ourselves persistently and unambiguously to our virtual avatars.

This could manifest as decentralised identity solutions where our real-life credentials map to avatar identities using blockchain identities, cryptographic proofs, biometrics and device telemetry. Verifiable reputations and personal attestations maintained on the blockchain could follow our avatars across virtual contexts.

Some metaverse experiences may require strict real-world identity proofing, while anonymity could be preserved in other environments via pseudonymous identities linked to digital wallets and fungible avatar representations. Regardless, the metaverse will need flexible identity frameworks balancing authentication, pseudonymity, privacy and continuity between worlds.

Experiencing Metaverse by visitors in a Tech-Metaverse exhibition in Middle East (Pic credit – Metaverse911)

Identity expression and representation in the metaverse transcends mere aesthetics into a crucial element of interactive presence across these interconnected realms. As we spend more time embodied as avatars within these spatial contexts, manifestations of our digital identities and associated artefacts will amass rich meaning and value.

In many ways, our metaverse avatars may become extensions of our very consciousness and mental imprint - acting as immersive surrogates to experience fantastic environments, garner reputations, proclaim affiliations, signal status, and ultimately, project our human existence across rapidly converging physical and virtual planes.

Chapter 10
Decentralisation and Blockchain in the Metaverse

In the vast digital expanse of the metaverse, where virtual worlds intertwine with our reality, decentralisation and blockchain technology stand as pillars of empowerment and innovation. As we delve into the tenth chapter of our exploration, we uncover the profound impact of decentralisation and blockchain in shaping the landscape of the metaverse.

Understanding Decentralisation in the Metaverse

Decentralisation lies at the heart of a transformative shift in how power is wielded within digital environments. Essentially, it disrupts the traditional hierarchy by dispersing authority and control across a network of participants rather than concentrating it in a central entity. When applied to the metaverse, decentralisation challenges the idea of a single governing body, ushering in a distributed ecosystem where users possess sovereignty over their digital assets, identities, and interactions.

Here's how it works: In traditional setups, like governments or corporations, power tends to be concentrated in the hands of a select few. However, decentralisation flips this paradigm by distributing control among a network of individuals or nodes. This means that decisions are no longer dictated by a central authority but rather emerge from the collective actions of participants.

Now, imagine applying this concept to the metaverse—a vast digital realm where virtual worlds intersect with our reality. Decentralisation in the metaverse dismantles the notion of a single governing entity, creating a landscape where users hold the reins over their digital lives. This empowers individuals to assert control over their virtual assets, identities, and interactions without reliance on intermediaries or centralised gatekeepers.

In essence, decentralisation in the metaverse represents a seismic shift in how we perceive authority and control within digital spaces. By dispersing power among participants and fostering a distributed ecosystem, it enables users to reclaim sovereignty over their digital existence, paving the way for a more democratic and inclusive virtual world.

Empowering Digital Ownership

Within the metaverse, decentralisation introduces a foundational principle known as digital ownership, reshaping how individuals interact with virtual assets. Utilising blockchain technology, users gain the ability to assert ownership rights over a myriad of virtual items, spanning from virtual real estate to in-game artefacts and digital artwork, all without the need for intermediaries. The immutable nature of blockchain's ledger ensures that transactions are transparent and secure, mitigating the risks associated with fraudulent activities and fostering trust within virtual economies.

Here's how it works: Imagine you acquire a valuable virtual item, like a rare sword in a game or a piece of digital artwork. Traditionally, proving ownership and transferring such assets could be cumbersome, often requiring the involvement of centralised entities. However, with blockchain technology, ownership rights are recorded on a decentralised and immutable ledger, eliminating the need for intermediaries. This means that you, as the owner, have complete control over your virtual assets, with the assurance that your ownership is securely recorded and cannot be tampered with.

Moreover, blockchain's transparency ensures that transactions within virtual economies are visible to all participants, enhancing trust and accountability. With each transaction securely recorded on the blockchain, users can verify the authenticity and ownership history of virtual assets, reducing the risk of scams or fraudulent activities.

In essence, empowering digital ownership through decentralisation revolutionises the way individuals engage with virtual assets within the metaverse. By leveraging blockchain technology, users gain autonomy over their virtual belongings, free from the constraints of centralised control. This not only promotes transparency and security within virtual economies but also fosters a sense of ownership and trust among participants, laying the groundwork for a thriving and equitable digital landscape.

Fostering Community Governance

In decentralised metaverse platforms, community governance mechanisms assume a crucial role in driving decision-making processes. Through consensus mechanisms like DAOs (Decentralised Autonomous Organizations), users collectively steer the trajectory of virtual worlds by voting on protocol upgrades and enforcing rules within the ecosystem. This democratised approach to governance promotes inclusivity and grants users the agency to actively shape their virtual environments.

Here's how it unfolds: Imagine a decentralised metaverse platform where users hold the power to influence the direction of virtual worlds. Instead of decisions being dictated by a central authority, governance mechanisms like DAOs enable users to participate in the decision-making process. Through DAOs, users can propose changes, vote on proposed upgrades, and enforce rules that govern the behaviour of participants within the ecosystem.

This democratised governance model ensures that decisions are made collectively, taking into account the diverse perspectives and interests of the community. By enabling users to have a say in how the metaverse evolves, it fosters a sense of inclusivity and empowerment, encouraging active engagement and participation.

Moreover, community governance mechanisms promote transparency and accountability within decentralised metaverse platforms. With decision-making processes being conducted openly and transparently, users can trust that their voices are heard and that governance decisions are made in the best interest of the community as a whole.

In essence, fostering community governance in the metaverse empowers users to take ownership of their virtual environments and actively contribute to their development. Through decentralised decision-making processes, users collectively shape the future of virtual worlds, ensuring that they remain inclusive, democratic, and reflective of the diverse interests and values of the community.

Ensuring Data Privacy and Security

In the metaverse, decentralisation serves as a cornerstone for both empowering users and safeguarding their privacy and security. By distributing data across a network of nodes rather than storing it in a centralised location, blockchain technology significantly reduces the risk of centralised data breaches and surveillance.

Here's how it operates: Imagine your data—such as personal information or transaction records—being stored on a distributed network of computers, known as nodes, rather than a single server controlled by a central authority. This decentralised approach makes it incredibly difficult for malicious actors to compromise or manipulate the data, as they would need to attack multiple nodes simultaneously, a task that is highly impractical and resource-intensive.

Moreover, blockchain employs cryptographic techniques such as zero-knowledge proofs and homomorphic encryption to further enhance privacy and security within the metaverse. Zero-knowledge proofs allow users to prove the validity of a statement without revealing any specific information, while homomorphic encryption enables computations to be performed on encrypted data without decrypting it, thus preserving confidentiality.

By leveraging these cryptographic methods, users can transact and communicate anonymously within the metaverse, safeguarding their digital identities from prying eyes. This ensures that individuals can engage in activities within virtual environments with confidence, knowing that their privacy and security are protected by design.

In summary, ensuring data privacy and security through decentralisation and cryptographic techniques is paramount in the metaverse. By decentralising data storage and implementing robust encryption methods, blockchain technology creates a secure and trustworthy environment where users can interact and transact freely without compromising their privacy or security. This fosters a sense of confidence and empowerment among users, paving the way for a vibrant and thriving digital ecosystem.

The Role of Blockchain Technology

Blockchain technology plays a pivotal role as the foundation of decentralisation in the metaverse, fundamentally reshaping how we engage with virtual environments. Through the utilisation of cryptographic principles and distributed consensus mechanisms, blockchain introduces a paradigm shift in the way transactions are conducted, digital identities are verified, and interoperability is achieved across various platforms.

Here's how it unfolds: Imagine blockchain technology as a decentralised ledger that records all transactions and data exchanges within the metaverse. Unlike traditional centralised systems, where a single authority controls the ledger, blockchain operates on a distributed network of computers, known as nodes. Each node maintains a copy of the ledger, ensuring transparency and integrity across the entire network.

Cryptographic principles, such as encryption and hashing, ensure that data stored on the blockchain is secure and tamper-proof. Transactions are cryptographically signed, making them immutable and resistant to unauthorised alterations. This not only enhances the security of virtual assets but also fosters trust among participants within the metaverse.

Furthermore, blockchain's distributed consensus mechanisms enable trustless transactions, eliminating the need for intermediaries or central authorities to validate transactions. Instead, consensus is reached through a network of nodes, ensuring that all transactions are validated and recorded transparently.

Another significant aspect of blockchain technology is its ability to facilitate verifiable digital identities. By leveraging cryptographic techniques, users can establish digital identities that are secure, tamper-proof, and interoperable across different platforms. This enhances trust and transparency within virtual environments, as users can verify the authenticity of digital identities and interactions.

Moreover, blockchain enables interoperability across disparate platforms within the metaverse. Through standardisation of protocols and cross-chain communication mechanisms, users can seamlessly transfer assets and data between different virtual worlds, fostering collaboration and innovation across the ecosystem.

In essence, the role of blockchain technology in the metaverse is transformative, revolutionising the way we perceive and interact within digital environments. By providing a secure, transparent, and interoperable foundation, blockchain empowers users to engage in trustless transactions, establish verifiable digital identities, and collaborate across virtual platforms, shaping a more vibrant and inclusive digital future.

Immutable Digital Records

At the core of blockchain technology lies its immutable nature, a feature that ensures once data is recorded on the blockchain, it remains unchanged and secure. This immutability is central to the integrity of virtual assets and transactions within the metaverse, providing users with indisputable evidence of ownership and authenticity.

Here's how it works: Picture the blockchain as a digital ledger that records all transactions and data exchanges within the metaverse. Each transaction is bundled into a block and added to the chain in a sequential and irreversible manner. Once a block is added to the chain, its contents are cryptographically hashed and linked to the previous block, creating a chain of blocks that forms a tamper-proof record of transactions.

This immutability ensures that once a transaction is recorded on the blockchain, it cannot be altered or deleted retroactively. This is because any attempt to tamper with a block would require altering the cryptographic hash of that block, which in turn would invalidate the entire chain, making it immediately apparent that tampering has occurred. As a result, users can trust that the information stored on the blockchain is accurate and reliable, providing a secure foundation for virtual asset ownership and transactions.

In practical terms, blockchain's immutability serves as a safeguard against fraud and manipulation within the metaverse. For example, when verifying the provenance of digital art, users can trace its history back to its original creation, confident that the information recorded on the blockchain is authentic and unaltered. Similarly, when tracking the lineage of virtual property, users can rely on the blockchain as a trusted ledger of truth, ensuring that ownership records remain transparent and immutable.

Overall, blockchain's immutable nature plays a vital role in maintaining the integrity and trustworthiness of virtual assets and transactions within the decentralised metaverse. By providing users with irrefutable proof of ownership and authenticity, blockchain serves as a reliable foundation for building a secure and transparent digital environment.

Interoperable Virtual Economies

Blockchain's interoperability broadens the horizons of virtual economies within the metaverse, facilitating seamless asset transfer across diverse platforms. It doesn't just end at securing transactions; it also breaks down barriers between different virtual worlds, creating a whole new frontier of possibilities. Imagine this scenario: you have virtual assets in one game or platform, but you want to use them in another. Before, that might have been tricky, like trying to use Monopoly money in a game of poker. But with blockchain's interoperability, it's like having a universal currency that you can use across various virtual realms.

Here's how it works: blockchain standardises protocols and employs cross-chain communication mechanisms to link up different metaverse platforms. Think of it as building bridges between different virtual worlds, allowing assets and value to flow freely between them. This interoperability not only enhances accessibility and liquidity but also fosters innovation as developers collaborate and leverage shared infrastructure.

Furthermore, interoperability serves as a catalyst for innovation. By enabling collaboration among developers across disparate platforms, it fosters an environment where new ideas can flourish and novel experiences can be created. This collaborative approach fuels creativity and enriches the virtual landscape for users.

Decentralised Identity and Reputation Systems

In the decentralised metaverse, fostering trust among users is essential. Blockchain-based identity and reputation systems play a pivotal role in this regard, empowering individuals to verify their identities and establish credibility within virtual communities. Through these systems, users can authenticate themselves securely and cultivate a reputation based on their interactions and contributions.

Here's how it works: imagine you're entering a virtual community or marketplace within the metaverse. Instead of relying on a centralised authority to vouch for your identity, you have the option to utilise a blockchain-based identity system. This system allows you to assert your identity using cryptographic techniques, ensuring that you are who you claim to be without compromising your privacy.

Additionally, reputation systems built on blockchain enable users to build trust over time through their actions and behaviours within the metaverse. Just like in the real world, positive interactions and contributions can enhance your reputation, while negative behaviours may detract from it. This creates a transparent environment where users can assess each other's credibility based on verifiable data rather than relying solely on subjective assessments.

One key aspect of these decentralised identity and reputation systems is self-sovereignty. This means that individuals have control over their personal data and can choose what information to disclose and to whom. By retaining ownership of their data, users can mitigate privacy concerns and foster a more secure environment within the metaverse.

In summary, decentralised identity and reputation systems in the metaverse serve to establish trust and credibility among users through secure authentication and transparent reputation mechanisms. By leveraging blockchain technology, individuals can assert their identities and cultivate their reputation based on their actions, all the while maintaining control over their personal data and privacy.

Embracing a Decentralised Future

As individuals navigate through the multifaceted landscapes of the metaverse, the principles of decentralisation and blockchain technology emerge as guiding forces, illuminating a trajectory towards a more equitable, transparent, and inclusive digital future. Embracing decentralisation entails a shift in power dynamics, empowering individuals to assert greater control over their digital identities and interactions within virtual realms.

Picture the metaverse as a vast digital universe where countless virtual worlds converge. In this dynamic environment, decentralisation serves as a beacon of empowerment, offering individuals the opportunity to reclaim ownership of their digital lives. By decentralising authority and dismantling centralised control structures, users are granted autonomy over their virtual assets, identities, and interactions.

But decentralisation isn't just about individual empowerment—it's also about fostering a more inclusive and collaborative digital ecosystem. By redistributing power among network participants, decentralisation facilitates a more democratic approach to decision-making and governance within virtual communities. This democratised ethos promotes transparency, accountability, and fairness, fostering an environment where diverse voices can contribute to the collective evolution of the metaverse.

At the heart of this decentralised future lies blockchain technology, a revolutionary tool that underpins trust and transparency in virtual environments. Through blockchain's immutable ledger and cryptographic principles, users can engage in trustless transactions, verify digital identities, and ensure the integrity of virtual assets.

By embracing decentralisation and blockchain technology, individuals are not only redefining social norms but also unlocking the full potential of virtual creativity and innovation. Freed from the constraints of centralised control, users can explore new avenues of expression, collaboration, and entrepreneurship within the metaverse.

In essence, the journey towards a decentralised future represents a paradigm shift in the way we conceptualise and interact with digital environments. It signifies a departure from top-down authority structures towards a more bottom-up, participatory approach wherein individuals wield greater agency and influence over their digital destinies. As we embrace the principles of decentralisation, we embark on a transformative voyage towards a digital future characterised by empowerment, inclusivity, and boundless innovation.

Democratising Access to the Metaverse

The concept of decentralisation plays a crucial role in democratising access to the metaverse, ensuring that participation is not restricted by centralised authorities or economic barriers. Through the adoption of open-source protocols and decentralised infrastructure, individuals from all walks of life gain the opportunity to engage with and contribute to the collective development of virtual worlds. This inclusive approach not only enhances the variety of experiences available within the metaverse but also cultivates a sense of community ownership and belonging among its participants.

Here's how it works: traditionally, access to virtual environments may have been limited by factors such as corporate control or financial constraints. However, decentralisation disrupts this paradigm by distributing control and decision-making power across a network of participants. This means that anyone with an internet connection and the desire to participate can join the metaverse, regardless of their background or financial status.

By embracing open-source protocols and decentralised infrastructure, the metaverse becomes more accessible and welcoming to a diverse range of individuals. This inclusivity not only fosters creativity and innovation but also promotes a sense of community ownership, where users feel empowered to shape the virtual world according to their preferences and interests.

In summary, decentralisation democratises access to the metaverse, opening up opportunities for individuals from all walks of life to contribute to and benefit from its collective evolution. This inclusive approach enriches the diversity of experiences within the metaverse and fosters a sense of belonging and community ownership among its participants.

Catalysing Innovation and Collaboration

Blockchain technology plays a pivotal role as a catalyst for innovation and collaboration within the metaverse ecosystem. By fostering an open and permissionless environment for experimentation, developers are empowered to iterate rapidly, explore new possibilities, and expand the horizons of virtual environments. Additionally, the decentralised nature of blockchain technology encourages collaboration across diverse disciplines, as creators, technologists, and visionaries come together to co-create the next wave of digital expression.

Here's how it works: blockchain technology provides a decentralised platform where developers can experiment freely without the constraints imposed by centralised authorities. This creates an environment conducive to innovation, where novel ideas can be explored and refined without bureaucratic hurdles. Developers can leverage blockchain's transparent and secure infrastructure to test new use cases, push the boundaries of technology, and pioneer groundbreaking advancements in virtual environments.

Moreover, blockchain's decentralised nature fosters collaboration among individuals from different backgrounds and expertise areas. Creators, technologists, and visionaries converge within the metaverse, drawn by the opportunity to collaborate on projects that transcend traditional boundaries. This interdisciplinary collaboration fuels creativity and drives innovation, as diverse perspectives and skill sets combine to shape the future of digital expression.

In summary, blockchain technology serves as a catalyst for innovation and collaboration within the metaverse ecosystem. By providing an open and permissionless platform for experimentation and fostering collaboration across disciplines, blockchain empowers developers to push the boundaries of what's possible in virtual environments and co-create a future defined by creativity, innovation, and digital expression.

Preserving Digital Sovereignty

In the current age of widespread surveillance and exploitation of personal data, decentralisation emerges as a sanctuary for digital sovereignty within the metaverse. By embracing principles such as privacy by design and encryption by default, decentralised platforms prioritise the protection of user rights and autonomy. This steadfast commitment to preserving digital sovereignty not only safeguards individual liberties but also cultivates a culture of trust and resilience in the face of evolving threats and challenges.

Here's how it works: In a centralised system, users often relinquish control of their data to a single authority, leaving them vulnerable to surveillance and potential exploitation. However, in a decentralised environment, users retain ownership and control over their data. Platforms are designed with privacy in mind from the outset, incorporating encryption techniques to ensure that user data remains confidential and secure.

This focus on preserving digital sovereignty not only protects individual rights but also fosters a sense of trust among users. Knowing that their data is protected and that they have control over how it is used instils confidence in the platform and encourages active participation.

Moreover, by prioritising digital sovereignty, decentralised platforms promote resilience in the face of emerging threats and challenges. With control distributed among users rather than concentrated in the hands of a single entity, decentralised systems are inherently less vulnerable to targeted attacks or data breaches. This resilience strengthens the overall integrity of the metaverse and ensures that users can engage with confidence in a secure and protected environment.

In summary, preserving digital sovereignty through decentralisation is essential for safeguarding individual liberties and fostering a culture of trust within the metaverse. By adhering to principles of privacy and encryption, decentralised platforms empower users to take control of their data and ensure their autonomy in the digital realm. This commitment not only protects against exploitation but also promotes resilience and trust in the face of evolving threats.

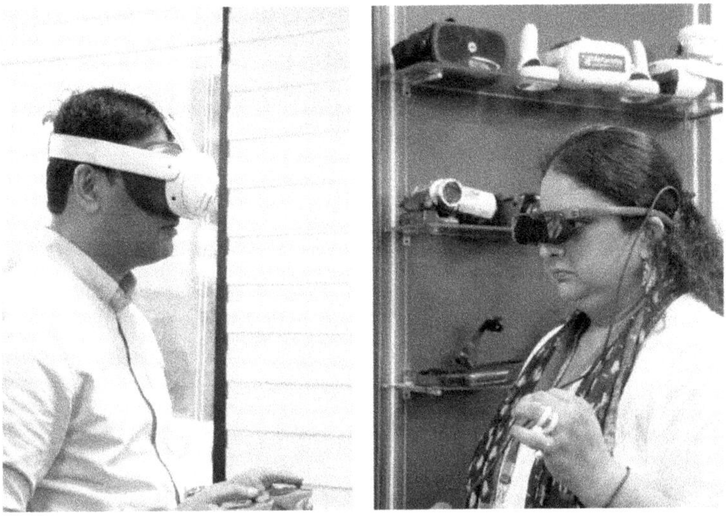

(Pic credit – Metaverse911)

Conclusion

As we conclude our exploration of decentralisation and blockchain in the metaverse, we stand at the precipice of a transformative paradigm shift in the way we perceive and interact with digital environments. By embracing the principles of decentralisation, we unlock a world of possibilities where autonomy, innovation, and inclusivity reign supreme. As pioneers of the decentralised metaverse, let us embark on this journey together, shaping a future where freedom and creativity know no bounds.

Chapter 11
Interoperability and Standards in the Metaverse

As the Metaverse continues to expand and evolve, one of the critical pillars supporting its growth is interoperability and the establishment of standards. In this chapter, we delve into the significance of interoperability, the challenges it presents, and the role of standards in shaping the future of virtual worlds.

Understanding Interoperability in the Metaverse

Interoperability refers to the ability of different systems, platforms, and applications to seamlessly communicate and exchange data with each other. In the context of the Metaverse, interoperability is essential for enabling users to move between various virtual environments, interact with diverse avatars, and access a wide range of content without encountering barriers.

In essence, interoperability fosters a unified and interconnected Metaverse where users can navigate effortlessly regardless of the platform they are on. Imagine being able to teleport from one virtual world to another with just a few clicks, bringing along your avatar, possessions, and social connections. This seamless experience is only possible through robust interoperability standards.

The Challenges of Interoperability

Navigating the vast expanse of the Metaverse presents a unique set of challenges, foremost among them being the quest for interoperability. In this digital realm, where virtual environments proliferate like galaxies in a cosmic expanse, achieving seamless communication and data flow between platforms is akin to navigating through a maze of disparate worlds.

A primary obstacle on this journey is the fragmentation inherent in the Metaverse. Picture it as a tapestry woven from countless threads, each representing a different virtual environment. These environments, whether bustling social hubs or immersive gaming realms, are crafted with their own distinct protocols, technologies, and standards. They operate as isolated islands, disconnected from one another, akin to separate realms in a vast universe.

This fragmentation creates what can be likened to silos—barriers that hinder the flow of information and assets between virtual worlds. Just as travellers may find it challenging to journey between distant lands separated by impassable terrain, users of the Metaverse encounter obstacles when attempting to traverse the boundaries between platforms. Assets created or acquired within one virtual environment may remain trapped within its confines, unable to freely roam the digital cosmos.

Yet, the challenges of interoperability extend beyond the mere technical realm. Imagine navigating a multilingual cityscape, where each district speaks its own unique dialect. Similarly, in the Metaverse, reconciling differences in user interfaces, interaction mechanisms, and content formats across platforms presents a formidable task. Achieving compatibility and consistency while respecting the diverse identities of each virtual world demands not only technical prowess but also collaboration and coordination among developers, stakeholders, and standards bodies.

In this quest for interoperability, developers and architects of the Metaverse must act as bridge-builders, spanning the chasms between virtual realms and forging connections that transcend boundaries. It is a journey fraught with challenges, yet brimming with possibilities. By embracing open standards, fostering collaboration, and nurturing a spirit of inclusivity, we can pave the way for a more interconnected and cohesive Metaverse—a digital frontier where users can roam freely, unencumbered by the shackles of platform boundaries.

The Role of Standards

In the intricate tapestry of the Metaverse, standards emerge as the guiding threads that weave together disparate realms into a cohesive digital landscape. These standards, akin to the common language spoken by diverse cultures, serve as the foundation upon which interoperability is built, fostering seamless communication and interaction across virtual environments.

At the heart of this endeavour lies the Extensible 3D (X3D) specification, a beacon of interoperability illuminating the path forward. Imagine it as a universal translator capable of deciphering the complexities of 3D content, enabling it to traverse the vast expanse of the Metaverse with ease. X3D's open-source nature and adaptable framework make it a cornerstone for fostering compatibility among virtual worlds, allowing users to navigate diverse environments without encountering linguistic barriers.

Similarly, initiatives such as the Open Metaverse Interoperability Protocol (OMIP) serve as bridges connecting the islands of the Metaverse, facilitating seamless communication and asset exchange between platforms. Think of OMIP as a common protocol shared by all, ensuring that regardless of the virtual realm one inhabits, users can interact and transact with ease. By adhering to OMIP standards, developers pledge allegiance to a shared vision of inclusivity and collaboration, laying the groundwork for a unified Metaverse ecosystem.

In essence, standards act as the glue binding together the diverse threads of the Metaverse, fostering interoperability and shaping its future landscape. Through collective effort and adherence to common principles, we can unlock the full potential of this digital frontier, ushering in an era where boundaries dissolve, and possibilities abound for all who venture forth into the boundless realms of the Metaverse.

Building Bridges Across Virtual Worlds

Interoperability not only benefits users by enhancing their virtual experiences but also presents opportunities for developers and businesses. By embracing interoperability standards, developers can tap into a larger ecosystem of users, assets, and services, expanding their reach and driving innovation.

For businesses, interoperability unlocks new possibilities for cross-platform marketing, advertising, and commerce. Imagine a virtual fashion brand that seamlessly integrates with multiple Metaverse platforms, allowing users to try on and purchase digital garments regardless of their virtual environment. Interoperability opens up a world of possibilities for monetisation and engagement in the Metaverse economy.

Overcoming Barriers to Interoperability

In the journey towards achieving full interoperability within the Metaverse, there are hurdles to surmount. One significant challenge arises from the reluctance of platform owners to relinquish their grip and adopt open standards. It's akin to envisioning a bustling city where each district insists on its own set of traffic rules, hindering smooth movement across the urban landscape.

Proprietary platforms, much like exclusive neighbourhoods, may resist interoperability efforts in a bid to safeguard their competitive edge and retain users within their walled gardens. Their reluctance to embrace open standards can create barriers that impede the free flow of data and assets between virtual worlds, akin to toll booths blocking the paths between districts.

Furthermore, ensuring the security, privacy, and integrity of data across interconnected virtual realms presents formidable technical and regulatory challenges. Picture it as safeguarding sensitive information as it traverses through a labyrinth of interconnected networks, where each passage poses its own set of risks and vulnerabilities.

To address these concerns, standards bodies and policymakers must collaborate closely with industry stakeholders to forge frameworks that strike a delicate balance between innovation and protection. It's akin to crafting a city-wide security protocol that safeguards the rights and interests of all residents while fostering an environment conducive to growth and collaboration.

By navigating these challenges with prudence and foresight, we can pave the way for a more inclusive and secure Metaverse—a digital realm where users can traverse freely, confident in the knowledge that their data and assets are safeguarded, and where innovation flourishes unhindered by the constraints of closed ecosystems.

Conclusion: Towards a Unified Metaverse

Interoperability and standards are indispensable components of the Metaverse's evolution, facilitating seamless navigation, collaboration, and innovation across virtual worlds. By embracing open standards and fostering interoperability, developers, businesses, and users can unlock the full potential of the Metaverse and build a more interconnected and inclusive digital realm.

As we embark on this journey towards a unified Metaverse, collaboration and cooperation will be key. By working together to define and uphold interoperability standards, we can create a vibrant and thriving virtual ecosystem where creativity knows no bounds, and users can explore, connect, and create without limitations. The future of the Metaverse is bright, and it's up to us to shape it into a world where everyone can belong and thrive.

Chapter 12
Privacy and Security in the Metaverse

In the bustling digital realm of the Metaverse, where reality intertwines seamlessly with virtuality, the notions of privacy and security takc on a new dimension. As we immerse ourselves deeper into this interconnected world of limitless possibilities, we must navigate the intricate web of safeguarding our personal information while fostering a secure environment for exploration and interaction. Chapter twelve of our journey through the Metaverse delves into the critical considerations of privacy and security, illuminating the pathways to safeguarding digital autonomy and protecting against emerging threats.

Understanding the Landscape

Before delving into the strategies and technologies aimed at fortifying privacy and security within the Metaverse, it is paramount to comprehend the landscape in which these principles operate. The Metaverse, an expansive digital universe comprising interconnected virtual environments, presents a multifaceted terrain where individuals traverse, interact, and create. From immersive social platforms to virtual marketplaces, every facet of the Metaverse is teeming with data exchanges and interpersonal engagements.

The Intersection of Privacy and Security

In the vast expanse of the Metaverse, privacy and security stand as fundamental principles, intertwined in their pursuit of preserving digital integrity. Yet, within this dynamic realm, they present both challenges and opportunities that require careful consideration.

Privacy, in essence, revolves around an individual's control over the dissemination and utilisation of their personal information. It's akin to having a lock on a diary, ensuring that only those authorised can access its contents. In the Metaverse, where interactions are myriad and data exchanges are constant, maintaining this control becomes paramount. It's about having the ability to decide what information to share, with whom, and for what purpose, akin to controlling the flow of personal details in a bustling digital marketplace.

On the other hand, security encompasses the protective measures put in place to prevent unauthorised access, breaches, and malicious activities. It's akin to having guards stationed around a fortress, safeguarding it from external threats. Within the Metaverse, where virtual assets are abundant and digital identities are at play, security ensures that these assets and identities remain intact and immune to nefarious actors seeking to exploit vulnerabilities. It's about building robust defences against cyber threats, such as hackers and malware, to ensure the safety and integrity of digital interactions and transactions.

Together, privacy and security form a symbiotic relationship, each reinforcing the other in their quest to uphold digital autonomy and protect against potential harm. In essence, privacy provides individuals with the agency to control their digital footprint, while security acts as a shield, safeguarding that footprint from unwanted intrusions.

Within the Metaverse, where virtual landscapes are vast and interconnected, navigating this intersection requires a nuanced understanding of the dynamics at play. It's about striking a balance between openness and protection, enabling individuals to freely explore and interact while ensuring that their rights and interests are safeguarded. Ultimately, it's about fostering an environment where trust, transparency, and empowerment rein supreme, laying the groundwork for a Metaverse that champions privacy, security, and digital well-being for all.

Nurturing Digital Autonomy

Central to the concept of privacy within the Metaverse is the notion of digital autonomy—a core principle that grants individuals the right to govern their virtual identity and data. It's akin to having the steering wheel in one's hands, allowing them to navigate their digital presence according to their own preferences and desires.

Empowering users with robust privacy controls and transparency mechanisms lies at the heart of nurturing digital autonomy. Picture it as having a dashboard in front of you, with switches and dials that enable you to customise your digital experience to your liking. Metaverse platforms play a crucial role in this endeavour by prioritising user-centric design, ensuring that individuals have the tools they need to safeguard their personal information.

This user-centric approach entails offering granular privacy settings, akin to having a sliding scale that allows you to adjust the level of privacy protection according to your comfort level. It's about giving users the ability to dictate who can access their data, how it can be used, and for what purposes. Moreover, clear consent mechanisms serve as signposts along the digital journey, ensuring that individuals are fully aware of and in control of the data they share.

In essence, nurturing digital autonomy in the Metaverse is about putting individuals firmly in the driver's seat of their digital destiny. It's about empowering them to make informed choices, exercise their rights, and assert their sovereignty over their personal information. By championing user empowerment and transparency, Metaverse platforms pave the way for a digital landscape where privacy is not just a privilege but a fundamental right—one that is accessible, respected, and protected for all.

Fortifying Cyber Defences

In the realm of the Metaverse, where digital landscapes flourish and virtual economies thrive, safeguarding against cyber threats becomes a critical imperative alongside preserving privacy. Imagine it as reinforcing the walls of a fortress to fend off potential invaders—strengthening the defences to protect against looming dangers.

As digital assets become more abundant and valuable, the temptation for malicious actors to exploit vulnerabilities grows exponentially. It's akin to treasure hunters eyeing a trove of riches, seeking to bypass any obstacles in their quest for ill-gotten gains. In response, fortifying cyber defences becomes paramount, akin to erecting barriers and deploying guards to ward off potential intruders.

One of the primary strategies in fortifying cyber defences within the Metaverse involves employing robust encryption protocols. Think of encryption as a secret code that renders data indecipherable to anyone without the proper key. By encrypting sensitive information, such as personal data and financial transactions, Metaverse platforms can thwart attempts by unauthorised parties to intercept and exploit such data.

Additionally, implementing multi-factor authentication mechanisms adds an extra layer of protection to digital identities within the Metaverse. It's like having a double-locked door that requires both a key and a passphrase to gain entry—an added hurdle for would-be attackers attempting to compromise accounts or access sensitive information.

In essence, fortifying cyber defences within the Metaverse is akin to building a sturdy fortress, equipped with layers of protection to safeguard against potential threats. By employing encryption and multi-factor authentication, Metaverse platforms bolster their resilience and mitigate the risks posed by cyber adversaries. It's about creating a digital landscape where users can explore, interact, and transact with confidence, knowing that their data and identities are safeguarded against the ever-present spectre of cyber threats.

Embracing Decentralisation and Blockchain

Decentralisation and blockchain technology serve as potent allies in safeguarding privacy and security within the Metaverse. They introduce a paradigm shift by distributing data across a network of nodes rather than storing it in a centralised location. This dispersal of data helps mitigate the risks associated with centralization, where a single breach can lead to catastrophic consequences.

Moreover, blockchain employs cryptographic mechanisms to ensure secure transactions, adding an extra layer of protection against unauthorised access and tampering. This enhances the integrity and transparency of transactions within the Metaverse, fostering trust among participants.

Smart contracts, a hallmark feature of blockchain technology, further bolster privacy by enabling automated, self-executing contracts without the need for intermediaries. These contracts execute predefined actions when certain conditions are met, facilitating trustless interactions and minimising the risk of fraud or manipulation.

Additionally, decentralised identity solutions offer a novel approach to managing digital identities within the Metaverse. By providing users with pseudonymous interactions and verifiable credentials, they enable individuals to assert control over their identity while preserving their privacy. This not only enhances security but also empowers users to navigate the digital landscape with confidence, knowing that their identity is protected against unauthorised access or misuse.

Fostering a Culture of Trust and Transparency

Fostering a culture of trust and transparency is essential for ensuring the privacy and security of users within the Metaverse. This involves more than just technological safeguards; it's about creating an environment where ethical data practices are prioritised. Platforms and communities must adhere to principles such as data minimisation, meaning they only collect the information necessary for a specific purpose, and purpose limitation, ensuring that data is only used for its intended purpose.

Transparent communication plays a vital role in building trust among users. By openly discussing data collection, storage, and utilisation practices, platforms can help users understand how their information is being handled. This transparency not only promotes trust but also fosters a symbiotic relationship between platform providers and participants, leading to a safer and more cooperative digital environment within the Metaverse.

Navigating Regulatory Frontiers

Navigating regulatory frontiers within the Metaverse is crucial as this digital landscape transcends geographical boundaries. It entails ensuring compliance with various legal frameworks governing data protection, cybersecurity, and digital rights. International standards and regulations serve as guiding principles for Metaverse platforms, dictating how data should be handled, secured, and used to uphold user privacy and security.

Collaborative efforts between policymakers, industry stakeholders, and civil society play a pivotal role in harmonising regulatory approaches across jurisdictions. By working together, they can address challenges such as jurisdictional conflicts and differing cultural norms, ultimately safeguarding user rights in the Metaverse. These collaborative endeavours are essential for fostering a regulatory environment that promotes innovation while ensuring the protection of individuals' digital rights and freedoms.

The Imperative of Continuous Innovation

The dynamic nature of the Metaverse necessitates a paradigm of continuous innovation in privacy and security practices. Threat landscapes evolve, technological advancements emerge, and societal norms shift—demanding agile responses and proactive strategies. From leveraging artificial intelligence for threat detection to integrating privacy-preserving technologies like homomorphic encryption, the pursuit of innovation is essential in staying ahead of emerging risks and vulnerabilities.

Conclusion

As we navigate the intricate nexus of privacy and security within the Metaverse, a collective endeavour emerges—one fuelled by the imperative of safeguarding digital autonomy and fostering a secure environment for collective flourishing. By embracing a holistic approach that encompasses technological fortifications, ethical principles, regulatory compliance, and innovative solutions, we chart a course forward towards a Metaverse that embodies the values of privacy, security, and trust.

Chapter 13
Education and Work in the Metaverse

As the Metaverse continues to evolve, its impact on education and work becomes increasingly profound. Chapter 13 delves into the transformative potentials of the Metaverse in these spheres. From immersive learning experiences to remote collaboration, the Metaverse is revolutionising how we acquire knowledge and engage in professional endeavours.

HoloAnatomy, an app developed by Case Western Reserve University and Cleveland Clinic, uses Microsoft's HoloLens augmented reality technology to teach anatomy to medical students.

Evolving Education in the Metaverse

Education within the Metaverse represents a departure from conventional learning methods, presenting a realm where traditional barriers such as physical distance and socioeconomic status are transcended. This evolution offers a dynamic and versatile learning environment, where immersive simulations, virtual classrooms, and interactive experiences redefine the very essence of education.

In this digital landscape, pedagogical approaches undergo a metamorphosis, catering to the diverse learning styles of individuals. Through the utilisation of personalised avatars, learners are not merely passive recipients of information but active participants in their educational journey. They engage in collaborative projects, simulations, and real-world scenarios, thereby fostering experiential learning that goes beyond the confines of textbooks and lectures.

Accessibility emerges as one of the most notable advantages of education within the Metaverse. Regardless of geographical location or socioeconomic background, individuals gain access to high-quality educational resources. Virtual libraries, museums, and educational hubs serve as repositories of knowledge, democratising access to information that was once confined to select institutions or geographic regions.

Moreover, the Metaverse fosters a culture of lifelong learning and upskilling, essential in an era defined by rapid technological advancement and economic evolution. Through gamified learning experiences and interactive modules, individuals embark on a journey of continuous growth, acquiring new skills and competencies that enhance their employability and adaptability in a dynamic job market.

The gamification of learning processes within the Metaverse injects an element of engagement and excitement, motivating learners to actively participate and progress. By transforming educational content into interactive experiences, individuals are empowered to explore, experiment, and learn at their own pace, thereby maximising their potential for mastery and retention.

Furthermore, the Metaverse serves as a hub for personalised learning experiences tailored to individual preferences and learning objectives. Adaptive algorithms and artificial intelligence algorithms analyse learner behaviour and preferences, customising educational content to meet their unique needs. This personalised approach not only enhances learning outcomes but also fosters a sense of empowerment and autonomy among learners.

Education within the Metaverse represents a paradigm shift in how we conceive, deliver, and engage with educational content. By transcending physical limitations and fostering accessibility, lifelong learning, and personalised experiences, the Metaverse holds the promise of democratising education and empowering individuals to realise their full potential in an ever-changing world.

Transforming Work Dynamics

Within the Metaverse, a profound transformation is underway in the realm of work, reshaping the way we collaborate, communicate, and conduct business. This shift represents a departure from traditional models, ushering in a new era of seamless and immersive remote work experiences.

Remote work within the Metaverse transcends the limitations of physical distance, offering virtual offices and meeting spaces that mirror their real-world counterparts. Through advanced technologies, teams collaborate in real-time, overcoming geographical boundaries and time zones to create a truly global workforce. This enables companies to harness talent from around the world, fostering diversity and innovation within their teams.

Central to this transformation is the integration of AI-driven assistants and virtual agents into work processes. These intelligent systems streamline workflows, enhancing productivity and efficiency across various domains, from project management to customer service. By automating repetitive tasks and providing valuable insights, AI augments human capabilities, driving innovation and competitiveness in the workplace.

Furthermore, the Metaverse serves as a catalyst for creativity and innovation through virtual co-creation spaces and design studios. Here, individuals from diverse backgrounds converge to ideate and innovate, fostering cross-disciplinary collaboration and synergy.

Virtual prototyping and simulations play a pivotal role in accelerating product development cycles, enabling companies to bring ideas to market faster and more efficiently.

This collaborative environment not only reduces time-to-market but also fosters iterative design processes, allowing for rapid experimentation and refinement. As a result, companies can adapt to changing market demands more effectively, staying ahead of the curve in an increasingly competitive landscape.

The Metaverse represents a paradigm shift in work dynamics, offering new possibilities for collaboration, creativity, and innovation. By leveraging advanced technologies and fostering a culture of remote work, companies can unlock new opportunities for growth and success in the digital age.

Metaverse Masterclass sessions at Metaverse99 studios based in Noida, India for educating industry professionals about different use-cases.

Challenges and Considerations

While the Metaverse holds immense promise for transforming education and work, it also presents a host of challenges and considerations that must be addressed to ensure its responsible and equitable development.

Digital literacy emerges as a critical concern in the Metaverse, as individuals must possess the necessary skills to navigate virtual environments safely and effectively. This entails not only technical proficiency but also an understanding of digital etiquette, privacy settings, and cybersecurity best practices. Without adequate digital literacy, users may be vulnerable to various online threats, including cyberbullying, phishing scams, and identity theft.

Moreover, concerns regarding data privacy, security, and digital rights management loom large in the Metaverse. As users interact and transact within virtual environments, they generate vast amounts of data that can be susceptible to exploitation or misuse. Robust frameworks and regulations are needed to safeguard individuals' rights and interests, ensuring that their personal information is protected and their digital identities remain secure.

Additionally, the digital divide persists as disparities in access to technology and connectivity hinder equitable participation in the Metaverse. While some individuals have access to high-speed internet and state-of-the-art devices, others may lack the necessary infrastructure or resources to fully engage in virtual environments. Bridging these gaps requires collaborative efforts from governments, businesses, and civil society to ensure inclusivity and accessibility for all.

Furthermore, ethical considerations surrounding AI, automation, and virtual identities demand careful examination in the Metaverse. The use of AI-driven algorithms and virtual agents raises concerns about algorithmic bias, as these systems may inadvertently perpetuate discriminatory outcomes or reinforce existing social inequalities. Additionally, the ethical use of personal data is paramount, as individuals' privacy rights must be respected and protected in virtual spaces.

To address these challenges, ethical frameworks must guide the development and deployment of Metaverse technologies, mitigating potential harms and promoting responsible innovation. Transparency, accountability, and user consent are essential principles that should underpin the design and implementation of virtual environments, ensuring that they uphold individuals' rights and values.

The Metaverse not only offers unprecedented opportunities for education and work, it also presents complex challenges that must be navigated thoughtfully and ethically. By addressing issues such as digital literacy, data privacy, and ethical considerations, we can harness the full potential of the Metaverse to create a more inclusive, equitable, and sustainable digital future.

Conclusion

In conclusion, the Metaverse heralds a new era in education and work, redefining how we learn, collaborate, and conduct business. From immersive learning experiences to virtual workplaces, its transformative potential is vast and multifaceted. However, realising this potential requires addressing challenges and considerations surrounding digital literacy, inclusivity, and ethics. By navigating these complexities thoughtfully, we can harness the full power of the Metaverse to create a more equitable, innovative, and interconnected world.

Chapter 14
Healthcare and Wellness in the Metaverse

The integration of healthcare services into the metaverse represents a significant advancement in the field of virtual reality (VR), augmented reality (AR), and mixed reality (MR) technologies. In this chapter, we explore how the metaverse is reshaping the healthcare landscape, offering innovative solutions for remote consultations, personalised wellness experiences, virtual therapy, and community support networks. By leveraging immersive technologies, data analytics, and peer networks, the metaverse is revolutionising healthcare delivery, promoting holistic well-being, and empowering individuals to take control of their health journey like never before.

The Evolution of Healthcare in the Metaverse

In recent years, the integration of healthcare services into the metaverse has witnessed remarkable growth, driven by advancements in immersive technologies and the increasing demand for remote and accessible healthcare solutions. Virtual healthcare platforms are redefining the patient experience, offering a wide range of services that were once confined to traditional brick-and-mortar settings. Through the seamless integration of VR, AR, and MR technologies, individuals can now access medical consultations, diagnostic assessments, and therapeutic interventions from the comfort of their homes. This shift towards virtual healthcare represents a fundamental transformation in how healthcare is delivered and experienced, with the potential to improve access, efficiency, and patient outcomes.

Virtual Hospitals and Clinics

The concept of virtual hospitals and clinics represents a departure from the conventional healthcare model, offering patients a novel way to engage with healthcare services. These virtual environments are designed to mimic the physical layout of traditional healthcare facilities, complete with waiting areas, examination rooms, and consultation spaces. Patients can navigate these virtual spaces using customizable avatars, interacting with digital representations of healthcare professionals and support staff. The immersive nature of these environments fosters a sense of presence and engagement, enhancing the overall patient experience. Additionally, virtual hospitals and clinics prioritise accessibility, catering to individuals with mobility limitations or those living in underserved areas with limited access to healthcare resources.

Personalised Wellness Experiences

Wellness initiatives in the metaverse are characterised by their focus on holistic approaches to physical and mental well-being. Virtual reality meditation apps, for example, transport users to serene landscapes, providing a tranquil escape from the stresses of daily life. These immersive experiences are designed to promote relaxation, mindfulness, and stress reduction, offering individuals a respite from the demands of modern living. Similarly, fitness programs leverage gamification and interactive experiences to motivate users to stay active and healthy. Whether it's through virtual yoga classes, guided meditation sessions, or gamified exercise routines, wellness experiences in the metaverse are tailored to individual preferences and goals, empowering users to take control of their health and well-being.

Health Monitoring and Data Analytics

The integration of wearable devices and biometric sensors into the metaverse enables real-time health monitoring and data analytics. From smartwatches to fitness trackers, these wearable technologies collect a wealth of physiological data, including heart rate, activity levels, and sleep patterns. Within virtual environments, users can access interactive dashboards and visualisations that provide insights into their health metrics. Advanced analytics algorithms analyse this data to identify trends, detect anomalies, and provide personalised recommendations for improving health outcomes. Whether it's tracking fitness goals, monitoring chronic conditions, or optimising sleep quality, health monitoring and data analytics in the metaverse empower individuals to make informed decisions about their health and well-being.

Virtual Reality Therapy and Rehabilitation

Virtual reality therapy is emerging as a promising approach for treating a wide range of mental health conditions and facilitating physical rehabilitation. By immersing patients in simulated environments, VR therapy offers a safe and controlled space for exposure therapy, cognitive-behavioural interventions, and relaxation techniques. For individuals with anxiety disorders, PTSD, or phobias, virtual reality exposure therapy allows them to confront their fears in a gradual and controlled manner, facilitating desensitisation and symptom reduction. Similarly, VR-based rehabilitation programs are enhancing traditional physical therapy approaches by providing interactive exercises, simulations, and feedback mechanisms. Whether it's recovering from a sports injury, regaining mobility after surgery, or managing chronic pain, virtual reality therapy and rehabilitation offer new avenues for improving functional outcomes and quality of life.

Community Support and Peer Networks

The metaverse provides a platform for fostering community support and peer networks among individuals facing similar health challenges. Virtual support groups bring together individuals with shared experiences, providing a space for mutual encouragement, empathy, and advice. Whether it's coping with a chronic illness, navigating mental health struggles, or recovering from a traumatic event, virtual support groups offer a sense of belonging and understanding. Peer networks empower individuals to share their knowledge, insights, and coping strategies, fostering a sense of solidarity and camaraderie. By connecting with others who understand their journey, individuals can find strength, resilience, and hope in the face of adversity.

Ethical Considerations and Privacy Concerns

As healthcare services become increasingly integrated with immersive technologies, ethical considerations and privacy concerns come to the forefront. Safeguarding patient confidentiality, ensuring data security, and mitigating the risks of unauthorised access are paramount. Virtual healthcare platforms must adhere to strict privacy regulations and security standards to protect sensitive medical information. Additionally, healthcare providers must be transparent about the risks and limitations of virtual healthcare services, ensuring that patients are informed and empowered to make decisions about their care. As the metaverse continues to evolve, it's essential to prioritise ethical principles, patient rights, and data privacy to build trust and confidence in virtual healthcare solutions.

Future Directions and Challenges

Looking ahead, the future of healthcare in the metaverse holds immense promise for innovation and transformation. Emerging technologies such as artificial intelligence, machine learning, and blockchain are poised to revolutionise healthcare delivery, diagnostics, and personalised medicine. Virtual reality telemedicine platforms will continue to expand access to healthcare services, particularly in underserved communities and remote regions. However, significant challenges remain, including digital inequality, regulatory barriers, and ethical considerations. Bridging the digital divide, ensuring equitable access to virtual healthcare services, and addressing concerns related to data privacy and security will be critical to realising the full potential of the metaverse in healthcare. By navigating these challenges thoughtfully and collaboratively, we can harness the transformative power of the metaverse to build a more accessible, inclusive, and patient-centred healthcare system for all.

Conclusion

Healthcare and wellness in the metaverse represent a convergence of cutting-edge technology and human-centric care. By leveraging immersive experiences, personalised interventions, and community support networks, the metaverse has the power to revolutionise healthcare delivery, promote holistic well-being, and empower individuals to lead healthier lives. As we navigate the complex terrain of the virtual realm, let us uphold ethical principles, prioritise patient-centred care, and harness the transformative potential of the metaverse to build a healthier and more inclusive future for all.

Chapter 15
Art, Creativity, and Expression in the Metaverse

The Metaverse, a convergence of virtual and augmented realities, is rapidly transforming how we interact, work, and express ourselves. This chapter explores how the Metaverse serves as a dynamic platform for art, creativity, and expression, highlighting practical examples, use cases, and the technologies driving these changes.

The Evolution of Art in the Metaverse

Digital Galleries and Virtual Museums

In the Metaverse, digital galleries and virtual museums have emerged as groundbreaking venues for showcasing art. For instance, platforms like VRChat and Spatial allow artists to create immersive galleries where visitors can interact with digital artworks in a 3D space. These virtual environments offer features such as:

- **Interactive Elements**: Users can engage with art pieces through touch or motion, triggering animations or sound effects.
- **Curated Experiences**: Artists can guide visitors through their work using VR tours, providing contextual information and interactive storytelling.

Case Study: The Museum of Other Realities (MOR)

The Museum of Other Realities is a notable example where artists exhibit their work in a fully immersive VR environment. This platform supports various digital formats, including 3D sculptures, virtual installations, and interactive media. By leveraging VR technology, MOR provides a space where art transcends physical limitations, allowing for more experimental and engaging exhibits.

Exploring the Boundaries of Creativity

Algorithmic and AI-Generated Art

Artificial Intelligence (AI) is revolutionising creative processes in the Metaverse. AI algorithms can generate complex art pieces, opening new avenues for artists. Tools like DALL-E and DeepArt use neural networks to create images based on textual descriptions or mimic the styles of famous artists.

Practical Example: AI Art Exhibitions

AI art exhibitions, such as those hosted by platforms like Art AI Gallery, showcase works generated by AI, challenging traditional notions of creativity and authorship. These exhibitions often feature pieces that blend human creativity with machine precision, offering a glimpse into the future of art creation.

Collaborative Art Projects

The Metaverse enables unprecedented levels of collaboration among artists. Using platforms like Decentraland and Cryptovoxels, artists can co-create in real-time, regardless of their physical locations. These virtual spaces support collaborative tools such as shared canvases and synchronised editing, facilitating seamless artistic cooperation.

Case Study: The Metaverse Art Week

Metaverse Art Week, hosted annually in Decentraland, exemplifies collaborative art in virtual spaces. This event brings together artists from around the world to create and showcase digital art installations, performances, and interactive experiences. By leveraging the Metaverse's collaborative capabilities, Art Week fosters a global community of creators.

The Intersection of Art and Technology

Augmented Reality (AR) Art

AR technology overlays digital content onto the physical world, creating hybrid experiences that blend real and virtual elements. Artists use AR to transform public spaces into interactive canvases, accessible through smartphones and AR glasses.

Practical Example: Pokémon GO Art Projects

Niantic's Pokémon GO has inspired various AR art projects, where artists use the game's AR features to create location-based installations. These projects demonstrate how AR can turn everyday environments into interactive art spaces, engaging a wider audience.

Blockchain and NFTs in Art

Blockchain technology and Non-Fungible Tokens (NFTs) are revolutionising the ownership and distribution of digital art. By leveraging blockchain's decentralised ledger system, NFTs provide a secure and transparent way to authenticate digital artworks. This technology ensures that each piece is unique and cannot be duplicated, offering a digital certificate of ownership that is verifiable by anyone.

NFTs allow artists to tokenise their digital creations, meaning they can sell, trade, and auction their work in digital marketplaces such as OpenSea and Rarible. This process not only helps artists retain control over their creations but also enables them to earn royalties each time their work is resold. The traceability of blockchain ensures that the provenance and history of the artwork are permanently recorded, which helps in verifying authenticity and maintaining value over time. This redefinition of art ownership empowers artists by providing new revenue streams and greater exposure, while also offering collectors a secure and transparent way to invest in digital art.

Use Case: Beeple's $69 Million NFT Sale

Digital artist Beeple made headlines with the $69 million sale of his NFT artwork "Everydays: The First 5000 Days" at Christie's. This event underscored the potential of NFTs to revolutionise the art market, offering artists new revenue streams and greater exposure.

The Social Impact of Art in the Metaverse

Raising Awareness and Social Issues

Artists in the Metaverse use their work to highlight social issues and drive change. Virtual installations and interactive experiences can address topics like environmental conservation, social justice, and mental health.

Practical Example: VR Climate Change Installations

Virtual reality installations focusing on climate change, such as those created by the group "This is Climate Change," immerse users in scenarios depicting the impacts of global warming. These experiences aim to educate and inspire action by offering a visceral understanding of environmental issues.

Empowering Marginalised Communities

The Metaverse democratises artistic expression, providing a platform for voices traditionally underrepresented in the art world. Virtual spaces enable artists from diverse backgrounds to share their stories and perspectives on a global stage.

Case Study: Virtual Indigenous Art Exhibits

Virtual galleries showcasing Indigenous art offer a platform for native artists to share their culture and history with a broader audience. These exhibits often include interactive elements and storytelling, providing deeper insight into Indigenous traditions and issues.

Technologies Driving Art in the Metaverse

Virtual Reality (VR)

VR creates fully immersive environments where users can interact with art in three dimensions. This technology is essential for virtual galleries, interactive installations, and immersive storytelling experiences.

Augmented Reality (AR)

AR integrates digital content with the physical environment, creating a more engaging experience by making interactions more dynamic and immersive. Artists use AR to create dynamic public art projects and interactive installations.

Artificial Intelligence (AI)

AI generates art through algorithms, offering new creative possibilities. AI tools can mimic styles, create original compositions, and even collaborate with human artists.

Blockchain and NFTs

Blockchain ensures the authenticity and provenance of digital art, while NFTs provide a mechanism for artists to monetise their work. These technologies are crucial for the emerging digital art market.

The Metaverse is a transformative arena for art, creativity, and expression, driven by cutting-edge technologies and innovative use cases. From AI-generated art to VR galleries and AR installations, the Metaverse offers a platform where creativity knows no bounds. As we continue to explore this digital frontier, the Metaverse will undoubtedly reshape the landscape of artistic expression, fostering a more inclusive, dynamic, and interconnected world.

Chapter 16
Legal and Ethical Considerations in the Metaverse

The Metaverse, an expansive digital universe that interconnects various virtual spaces, presents numerous opportunities for innovation and interaction. As this ecosystem grows, it introduces complex legal and ethical challenges. Navigating these considerations is crucial for fostering a safe, equitable, and sustainable Metaverse. This chapter explores the multifaceted legal and ethical issues that stakeholders must address, including regulatory frameworks, intellectual property rights, privacy, data security, digital identity, and broader societal impacts.

Regulatory Frameworks

- **Existing Laws and New Challenges:** The Metaverse's rapid development outpaces existing legal frameworks, which were not designed to handle virtual environments. Traditional laws regarding property, contracts, and consumer protection need adaptation to address virtual goods and services. For instance, determining jurisdiction in a decentralised Metaverse can be complex, as transactions and interactions occur across global networks.

- **International Cooperation:** Given the global nature of the Metaverse, international cooperation is essential. Countries must collaborate to create harmonised regulations that prevent legal conflicts and ensure consistent standards. International bodies, such as the United Nations or the World Economic Forum, could play pivotal roles in facilitating these discussions and establishing global guidelines.

Intellectual Property Rights

- **Ownership of Digital Assets:** Intellectual property (IP) rights are a significant concern in the Metaverse, where digital assets such as virtual real estate, avatars, and non-fungible tokens (NFTs) are prevalent. Clarifying ownership rights and enforcement mechanisms is crucial to protect creators and users. Blockchain technology can provide transparent and immutable records of ownership, but legal systems must recognise and uphold these digital records.

- **Copyright and Fair Use:** The ease of copying and distributing digital content in the Metaverse raises concerns about copyright infringement. Laws must balance protecting creators' rights with allowing fair use, which is vital for innovation and expression. The implementation of digital rights management (DRM) systems can help control unauthorised use, but these must be carefully designed to avoid overreach and respect users' rights.

Privacy and Data Security

- **Data Collection and Consent:** In the Metaverse, vast amounts of personal data are collected through interactions and transactions. Ensuring users' informed consent and control over their data is paramount. Privacy policies must be transparent and easily understandable, outlining what data is collected, how it is used, and with whom it is shared. Technologies like decentralised identifiers (DIDs) and zero-knowledge proofs can enhance user privacy and data security.

- **Protecting Minors:** Children and adolescents are significant users of virtual environments, necessitating robust protections against data exploitation and inappropriate content. Age verification systems and parental controls should be implemented to safeguard young users, and regulations must enforce stringent penalties for violations.

Digital Identity and Reputation

- **Identity Verification:** Verifying digital identities in the Metaverse presents unique challenges. Users often create avatars that may not reflect their real-world identities, complicating efforts to ensure accountability and prevent fraud. Developing reliable identity verification systems that respect user anonymity while ensuring trust and safety is essential.

- **Reputation Management:** Reputation systems can help build trust in the Metaverse by providing information about users' past behaviours. However, these systems must be designed to prevent abuse and ensure fairness. Transparent algorithms and mechanisms for users to contest and correct their reputations are necessary to avoid unjust outcomes.

Ethical Considerations

- **Equity and Inclusion:** The Metaverse must be accessible and inclusive, avoiding the perpetuation of existing social inequalities. Efforts should focus on providing equal access to technology, combating digital divides, and ensuring diverse representation. Inclusive design principles and proactive policies can help achieve these goals.

- **Content Moderation:** Moderating content in the Metaverse is challenging due to the sheer volume and diversity of user-generated content. Effective moderation requires a combination of automated tools and human oversight. Ethical considerations include respecting freedom of expression while preventing harm, such as harassment, hate speech, and misinformation. Transparent moderation policies and user appeals processes are crucial for fairness and accountability.

- **Virtual Harassment and Abuse:** Virtual environments can be breeding grounds for harassment and abuse, necessitating robust measures to protect users. Clear policies against abusive behaviour, effective reporting mechanisms, and support systems for victims are essential. Legal frameworks must also address these issues, ensuring perpetrators are held accountable and victims have recourse.

Societal Impacts

- **Economic Disparities:** The Metaverse has the potential to create new economic opportunities but also risks exacerbating existing disparities. Ensuring that economic benefits are widely distributed requires policies that support equitable access to digital resources and opportunities. Education and training programs can help individuals from diverse backgrounds participate in and benefit from the Metaverse economy.

- **Mental Health and Well-being:** The immersive nature of the Metaverse can impact users' mental health and well-being. While it offers opportunities for social connection and creative expression, it can also lead to issues such as addiction, social isolation, and identity confusion. Ethical considerations include promoting healthy usage patterns, providing resources for mental health support, and designing environments that foster positive experiences.

Future Prospects and Legal Evolution

- **Adaptive Legal Frameworks:** As the Metaverse evolves, so too must the legal frameworks that govern it. Laws need to be adaptive and forward-thinking, anticipating future developments and challenges. Regular reviews and updates of regulations, informed by ongoing research and stakeholder input, are essential for keeping pace with technological advancements.

- **Ethical Leadership and Governance:** Ethical leadership and governance are crucial for guiding the Metaverse's development. Stakeholders, including developers, policymakers, and users, must collaborate to establish ethical guidelines and governance structures that prioritise the common good. This includes fostering a culture of responsibility, transparency, and accountability across the ecosystem.

Navigating the legal and ethical landscape of the Metaverse is a complex and ongoing endeavour. As this digital frontier continues to expand, it is imperative to develop robust regulatory frameworks and ethical guidelines that ensure a safe, inclusive, and equitable environment for all users. By addressing these challenges proactively and collaboratively, stakeholders can harness the full potential of the Metaverse while safeguarding fundamental rights and values.

Chapter 17
Sports and Fitness in the Metaverse

As the metaverse evolves, its application in various sectors continues to expand, with sports and fitness emerging as a dynamic frontier. This chapter explores how the integration of sports, fitness, and the metaverse is reshaping the way we engage with physical activities, athletic training, and even sporting events. By blending physical and digital experiences, the metaverse is transforming sports and fitness into more interactive, accessible, and personalised activities.

Virtual Sports and Training Environments

One of the most significant impacts of the metaverse on sports is the creation of virtual training environments. Athletes can now practice and refine their skills in realistic, simulated settings without the need for physical facilities. These virtual environments can replicate a variety of conditions, from football fields to basketball courts, allowing athletes to train anytime, anywhere.

Advanced motion tracking and virtual reality (VR) technology enable athletes to receive real-time feedback on their movements and techniques. For instance, a golfer can analyse their swing through VR, with data-driven insights helping them improve their performance. Similarly, football players can practice strategic plays and scenarios in a virtual stadium, enhancing their tactical understanding and reflexes.

Immersive Spectator Experiences

The metaverse also offers unprecedented opportunities for sports enthusiasts to engage with their favourite teams and events. Virtual stadiums and arenas are being developed where fans can watch live games from the comfort of their homes, with a sense of presence that traditional broadcasting cannot replicate. These virtual venues provide a 360-degree view of the action, allowing fans to choose their vantage points, interact with other spectators, and even participate in pre- and post-game activities.

In addition to live games, virtual reality allows fans to relive historic matches or experience legendary sporting moments from a first-person perspective. This immersive engagement creates deeper connections between fans and their favourite sports, enhancing the overall spectator experience.

Personalised Fitness and Wellness Programs

Fitness and wellness are integral aspects of the metaverse, with virtual reality fitness applications offering personalised workout programs tailored to individual needs. These applications can simulate a range of fitness activities, from yoga and pilates to high-intensity interval training (HIIT) and virtual cycling. Users can exercise in diverse, visually stimulating environments, from serene beaches to futuristic cities, keeping workouts engaging and enjoyable.

Wearable technology, integrated with the metaverse, tracks users' performance metrics such as heart rate, calories burned, and steps taken. This data is used to tailor fitness programs further, providing real-time feedback and personalised coaching. Virtual personal trainers guide users through their routines, ensuring proper form and motivation, much like an in-person trainer.

Social and Competitive Aspects

The metaverse enhances the social dimension of sports and fitness by enabling users to participate in group workouts, challenges, and competitions. Virtual fitness classes allow users from different parts of the world to exercise together, fostering a sense of community and camaraderie. Competitive features such as leaderboards, virtual races, and fitness challenges motivate participants to push their limits and achieve their goals.

Esports and virtual sports leagues have also gained traction, with players competing in digital arenas for both fun and professional accolades. These events attract large audiences and generate substantial revenue, further solidifying the role of the metaverse in the sports industry.

Accessibility and Inclusivity

One of the most transformative aspects of the metaverse is its potential to make sports and fitness more accessible. Virtual environments can be customised to accommodate individuals with physical disabilities, offering adaptive fitness programs that cater to their specific needs. This inclusivity allows a broader audience to participate in and enjoy physical activities, promoting a healthier and more active lifestyle for all.

Latest Practical Applications of the Metaverse in Sports

1. Virtual Training and Performance Analysis

- **STRIVR**: A leading brand in VR sports training, STRIVR offers virtual reality platforms used by professional teams in the NFL, NBA, and other leagues to simulate game scenarios and improve player performance. Athletes can practice strategic plays and receive real-time feedback, helping them enhance decision-making and reaction times.

- **Rezzil**: A VR training platform widely used by football clubs to help players improve cognitive skills, reaction times, and decision-making under pressure. Rezzil's platform offers drills that replicate real match situations, providing data-driven insights for performance improvement.

2. Immersive Fan Experiences

- **NextVR (acquired by Apple)**: NextVR has been pioneering live-streaming of sports events in virtual reality. Fans can experience live games as if they are in the stadium, choosing their vantage point and interacting with other viewers virtually.

- **Sony's Hawk-Eye Innovations**: Known for its application in tennis and football, Hawk-Eye's immersive replay technology enhances the viewing experience by allowing fans to view games from any angle in 3D, offering a new level of engagement.

NextVR provides profound immersion to put you right in the action for NBA games, WWE, boxing, NHRA, ICC soccer, concerts, behind-the-scenes music experiences and stand-up comedy events. You can even explore haunted locations with Paranormal Evidence and other award-winning NextVR Originals.

3. Fitness and Wellness

- **Supernatural VR**: This VR fitness platform offers immersive workout experiences in stunning virtual environments, ranging from serene beaches to ancient temples. It combines cardio, strength training, and mindfulness, providing users with guided workouts and real-time feedback through VR headsets like Oculus Quest.

- **Peloton's VR Integration**: Peloton is exploring virtual reality to offer more immersive cycling and fitness classes. Users can participate in virtual cycling races or fitness challenges, adding a gamified layer to their workouts.

Supernatural VR Boxing MR Games

4. Esports and Virtual Competitions

- **Zed Run**: A blockchain-based horse racing game, Zed Run allows users to own, breed, and race virtual horses. The platform combines elements of traditional sports, gaming, and cryptocurrency, offering a unique metaverse experience for sports enthusiasts.

- **Sorare**: A fantasy football game that uses blockchain technology to create a global fantasy league. Players buy, sell, and trade officially licensed player cards as NFTs, engaging in virtual football competitions.

Zed Run, the exciting digital horse racing universe where players can own, breed, and race their unique digital racehorses.

5. **Virtual Memorabilia and Fan Tokens**

- **Socios.com**: A platform that enables sports teams to issue fan tokens on the blockchain. These tokens allow fans to participate in team decisions, earn rewards, and access exclusive content. Major football clubs like FC Barcelona, Juventus, and Paris Saint-Germain have embraced Socios.com to deepen fan engagement.

- **NBA Top Shot**: Developed by Dapper Labs, NBA Top Shot allows fans to buy, sell, and trade officially licensed NBA highlight clips as NFTs. This has created a new form of digital memorabilia, blending the worlds of sports and blockchain technology.

6. Virtual Stadiums and Events

- **Decentraland**: This decentralised virtual world platform has hosted virtual sports events and partnered with various sports organisations to create interactive experiences. Fans can visit virtual stadiums, meet players, and participate in exclusive events. For example, Snoop Dogg hosted a virtual concert, allowing fans to attend a live show and interact with others in real-time. Atletico Madrid created a virtual fan zone where supporters could watch matches and engage with the team's history. Paris Hilton showcased her NFT art collection in a virtual gallery, blending fashion, art, and VR. Additionally, DJ Deadmau5 held a virtual performance, providing fans with an immersive experience through live music and interactive visuals.

- **Manchester City's Virtual Stadium**: Manchester City is collaborating with Sony to build a virtual replica of their Etihad Stadium. This initiative aims to offer fans a virtual venue where they can watch games, interact with fellow supporters, and participate in events, regardless of their physical location.

7. Gadgets and Technologies

VR Headsets

- **Oculus Quest 2**: A leading VR headset that provides a wireless, immersive experience for gaming, fitness, and sports applications. It is widely used for platforms like Supernatural and VR sports training.

- **HTC Vive Pro**: Known for its high-resolution display and robust tracking, HTC Vive Pro is used in various sports training and fitness applications, offering an immersive experience for users.

Wearable Technology

- **FitXR**: A VR fitness app that tracks user performance, including heart rate and calories burned, using wearable devices like smartwatches. This integration ensures users get comprehensive feedback on their workouts.

- **WHOOP Strap**: A fitness wearable that provides detailed insights into recovery, sleep, and performance. Athletes use WHOOP to monitor their readiness for training, with data being integrated into virtual training programs within the metaverse.

The Future of Sports in the Metaverse

The integration of sports and fitness into the metaverse is still in its early stages, but the potential for growth is immense. Future developments may include more sophisticated VR hardware, enhanced motion capture technology, and AI-driven personal trainers that offer highly personalised and adaptive coaching.

Moreover, as blockchain technology and non-fungible tokens (NFTs) gain prominence, virtual sports memorabilia, player avatars, and even virtual real estate in sports-themed worlds may become valuable assets. This convergence of technology and sports will continue to blur the lines between physical and virtual experiences, creating a new paradigm for how we engage with sports and fitness.

Conclusion

The metaverse is poised to revolutionise the sports and fitness industry by providing immersive, interactive, and accessible experiences. From virtual training environments and personalised fitness programs to engaging spectator experiences and social interactions, the metaverse offers endless possibilities for athletes, fans, and fitness enthusiasts. As technology continues to evolve, the role of the metaverse in sports and fitness will undoubtedly expand, offering innovative ways to stay active, connected, and entertained.

Chapter 18
Future Prospects and Challenges of the Metaverse

As we reach the final chapter of our exploration into the metaverse, it is essential to look ahead at the future prospects and challenges that will shape this rapidly evolving digital frontier. The metaverse, a convergence of virtually enhanced physical reality and physically persistent virtual space, represents a paradigm shift in how we interact with technology, one another, and the world around us. In this chapter, we will discuss the potential future developments within the metaverse, the opportunities it presents, and the challenges that must be addressed to ensure a sustainable and inclusive digital ecosystem.

Future Prospects of the Metaverse

- **Technological Advancements**

The metaverse is poised for exponential growth, driven by continuous technological advancements. The development of more sophisticated and accessible hardware, such as lightweight AR glasses and more immersive VR headsets, will significantly enhance user experiences. Improvements in computing power, network infrastructure, and AI will enable more complex and realistic virtual environments. Emerging technologies like 5G and edge computing will reduce latency, facilitating seamless real-time interactions.

- **Integration with AI and Machine Learning**

AI and machine learning will play a crucial role in the evolution of the metaverse. AI-driven avatars, capable of understanding and responding to human emotions and behaviours, will create more natural and engaging interactions. Machine learning algorithms will optimise virtual environments based on user preferences and behaviours, making experiences more personalised and immersive. Additionally, AI can facilitate content creation, automating the development of vast and diverse virtual landscapes.

- **Expansion of Virtual Economies**

The metaverse will likely see the continued expansion of virtual economies. Cryptocurrencies and NFTs will become increasingly integral, enabling secure and transparent transactions. Virtual real estate, digital fashion, and other forms of digital goods and services will proliferate, creating new markets and economic opportunities. This digital economy will not only benefit individual users but also drive innovation and growth in various industries, including entertainment, retail, and real estate.

- **Interoperability and Standardisation**

One of the critical prospects for the metaverse is the development of interoperability and standardisation. Currently, the metaverse comprises numerous disparate platforms and ecosystems. For the metaverse to achieve its full potential, seamless interaction between these platforms is essential. Standardised protocols and frameworks will facilitate cross-platform interactions, allowing users to move their assets, identities, and experiences seamlessly across different virtual environments. This interoperability will drive user adoption and create a more cohesive and inclusive digital ecosystem.

- **Enhanced Social Interactions**

The metaverse holds the promise of revolutionising social interactions. Virtual gatherings, from casual meetups to large-scale events, will become more immersive and engaging. Social VR platforms will enable users to interact in ways that mimic real-life social dynamics, fostering deeper connections and collaboration. As the metaverse becomes more integrated into daily life, it will offer new opportunities for socialisation, entertainment, and community building, transcending geographical boundaries.

- **Educational and Professional Opportunities**

The metaverse has the potential to transform education and work. Virtual classrooms and training environments will offer interactive and experiential learning opportunities, making education more accessible and engaging. In the professional realm, virtual offices and collaborative workspaces will enable remote teams to work together more effectively. The metaverse will also create new job opportunities, from virtual real estate agents to digital fashion designers, expanding the scope of employment possibilities.

Challenges of the Metaverse

- **Technical and Infrastructure Challenges**

Despite the promising prospects, the metaverse faces significant technical and infrastructure challenges. Developing the necessary hardware and software to support large-scale, immersive virtual environments requires substantial investment and innovation. Ensuring reliable and high-speed connectivity, particularly in underserved regions, is critical for widespread adoption. Moreover, the energy consumption of large data centres and blockchain technologies poses environmental concerns that need to be addressed.

- **Privacy and Security Concerns**

Privacy and security are paramount in the metaverse. As users engage in more complex and intimate interactions, protecting their data and digital identities becomes increasingly challenging. The potential for data breaches, cyber-attacks, and identity theft is significant. Establishing robust security protocols and regulatory frameworks is essential to safeguard user information and maintain trust. Additionally, addressing issues related to surveillance, data ownership, and consent is crucial to creating a secure and ethical metaverse.

- **Ethical and Legal Considerations**

The metaverse raises numerous ethical and legal questions. Issues such as digital equity, access, and inclusion must be addressed to prevent the digital divide from widening. Ensuring that all individuals, regardless of socio-economic status or geographical location, can participate in and benefit from the metaverse is essential. Legal frameworks must also evolve to address new forms of digital property, intellectual property rights, and virtual crime. Balancing innovation with ethical considerations will be key to creating a fair and just metaverse.

- **Societal and Cultural Impacts**

The metaverse will have profound societal and cultural impacts. It will reshape how we perceive reality, identity, and community. While it offers new opportunities for connection and expression, it also poses risks of social isolation, addiction, and mental health issues. Understanding and mitigating these risks will be essential to ensuring that the metaverse enhances, rather than detracts from, our well-being. Moreover, fostering cultural diversity and representation within the metaverse is crucial to creating inclusive and vibrant virtual communities.

- **Economic Disparities**

The economic potential of the metaverse could exacerbate existing disparities. While it creates new opportunities for wealth generation, there is a risk that the benefits will be unevenly distributed. Ensuring that the economic gains of the metaverse are accessible to a broad range of participants, rather than being concentrated among a few large corporations or affluent individuals, is vital. Developing policies and initiatives that promote equitable access and participation will help address these economic challenges.

- **Environmental Sustainability**

The environmental impact of the metaverse cannot be overlooked. The infrastructure required to support virtual environments, from data centres to blockchain networks, consumes significant energy. As the metaverse grows, finding sustainable solutions to mitigate its environmental footprint will be critical. This includes developing energy-efficient technologies, utilising renewable energy sources, and implementing policies that promote environmental responsibility within the digital ecosystem.

Conclusion

The metaverse represents a bold new frontier in the digital age, offering unprecedented opportunities for innovation, connection, and economic growth. However, realising its full potential requires addressing a range of technical, ethical, and societal challenges. By fostering collaboration between stakeholders, including technologists, policymakers, and the public, we can shape a metaverse that is secure, inclusive, and sustainable.

As we conclude our exploration of the metaverse, it is clear that this digital realm is not just a technological marvel but a reflection of our collective aspirations and values. The future of the metaverse will be defined by our ability to navigate its complexities and harness its potential for the greater good. By prioritising ethical considerations, ensuring equitable access, and embracing sustainable practices, we can create a metaverse that enriches our lives and fosters a more connected and inclusive world. The journey into the metaverse is just beginning, and its future will be shaped by the choices we make today.

GLOSSARY

1. **Airdrop**
   Free distribution of tokens to promote a project.
   Example: Uniswap airdropped tokens to early users.

2. **Artificial Intelligence (AI)**
   Simulation of human intelligence by machines for tasks like learning and decision-making.
   Example: AI powers non-player characters (NPCs) in virtual worlds.

3. **Augmented Reality (AR)**
   A technology that overlays digital images, sounds, or other sensory data onto real-world environments, creating an interactive and immersive experience through devices such as smartphones and wearable AR glasses.
   Example: Pokémon Go revolutionised AR gaming.

4. **Augmented Spaces**
   Physical locations enhanced by augmented reality technology.
   Example: Museums using AR to provide interactive tours.

5. **Avatar**
   A customised digital figure or character used by a person to represent themselves in online or virtual environments.
   Example: Roblox allows users to customise avatars extensively.

6. **Blockchain**
   A decentralised ledger technology used for secure and transparent record-keeping.
   Example: Ethereum powers smart contracts and NFTs.

7. **Blockchain Ecosystem**
   A network of blockchain platforms, applications, and services.
   Example: Binance Smart Chain is part of the blockchain ecosystem.

8. **Blockchain Interoperability**
   Ability for blockchains to share data and assets.
   Example: Polkadot enables communication between multiple blockchains.

9. **Consensus Mechanism**
   The process by which blockchain networks validate transactions.
   Example: Proof of Stake (PoS) is a popular mechanism in Ethereum 2.0.

10. **Creator Economy**
    Ecosystem allowing individuals to monetise content.
    Example: Patreon supports creators across various platforms.

11. **Crowdfunding**
    Raising funds online, often through decentralised platforms.
    Example: Kickstarter supports creators with funding opportunities.

12. **Cryptocurrency**
    Digital currency secured by cryptography and used for transactions in virtual economies.
    Example: Bitcoin and Ethereum are leading cryptocurrencies.

13. **DAO (Decentralised Autonomous Organisation)**
    A member-driven entity governed by smart contracts.
    Example: MakerDAO manages the DAI stablecoin ecosystem.

14. **Decentralisation**
    Distribution of data and control away from central authorities.
    Example: Filecoin enables decentralised file storage.

15. **DeFi (Decentralised Finance)**
    Financial services powered by blockchain and smart contracts.
    Example: Aave enables decentralised lending and borrowing.

16. **Digital Asset**
    Any content or value stored in a digital format.
    Example: Cryptocurrencies and NFTs are digital assets.

17. **Digital Collectibles**
    Virtual items with unique properties and ownership.
    Example: Iconic basketball highlights are sold as NFTs by NBA Top Shot, enabling fans to own these unique digital assets.

18. **Digital Ecosystem**
    Interconnected platforms and services within a Metaverse.
    Example: Meta integrates Horizon Worlds, VR headsets, and NFTs.

19. **Digital Identity**
    A user's representation in virtual ecosystems.
    Example: ENS (Ethereum Name Service) allows blockchain-based identities.

20. **Digital Ledger**
    A secure, digital record of transactions.
    Example: Bitcoin's blockchain is a decentralised ledger.

21. **Digital Marketplace**
    A platform for trading digital assets.
    Example: Rarible is a marketplace for NFTs.

22. **Digital Sovereignty**
    Users' control over their digital assets and data.
    Example: Sovrin provides self-sovereign identity solutions.

23. **Digital Twin**
    A virtual replica of a physical object or system for simulation and analysis.
    Example: BMW uses digital twins for factory planning.

24. **Edge Computing**
    Processing data near its source to reduce latency.
    Example: Meta uses edge computing to enhance VR performance.

25. **Gas Fees**
    Costs associated with blockchain transactions.
    Example: High Ethereum gas fees drive users to Layer 2 solutions.

26. **Governance Token**
    Tokens granting holders voting rights within a project.
    Example: UNI token holders can vote on Uniswap proposals.

27. **Hashing**
    Cryptographic process of converting data into fixed strings.
    Example: Bitcoin uses SHA-256 for hashing transactions.

28. **Haptic Feedback**
    Touch-based feedback in digital interactions.
    Example: Haptic gloves allow tactile experiences in VR.

29. **Immersive Content**
    Media designed for AR, VR, or MR environments.
    Example: The VR film "Spheres" provides an immersive

storytelling experience.

30. **Immersive Storytelling**
    Narratives experienced through AR or VR technologies.
    Example: "The Line" is a VR story available on Oculus.

31. **In-Game Assets**
    Items within video games that hold value.
    Example: CryptoKitties' digital cats are tradeable assets.

32. **Interactivity**
    The ability to engage and manipulate digital content.
    Example: Interactive VR games like Beat Saber.

33. **Interoperability**
    The ability of systems to work seamlessly across platforms.
    Example: Decentraland supports NFTs from other blockchain platforms.

34. **IoT (Internet of Things)**
    Devices interconnected through the internet, enabling data exchange.
    Example: Smart thermostats integrating with VR homes.

35. **Layer 2 Solutions**
    Technologies built atop blockchain networks to enhance scalability.
    Example: Polygon offers Layer 2 solutions for Ethereum.

36. **Liquidity Pool**
    A reserve of cryptocurrencies for decentralised trading.
    Example: Uniswap's liquidity pools enable token swaps.

37. **Metaverse**
    A collective virtual space where users interact, work, and play.
    Example: Meta's Horizon Worlds is a growing Metaverse platform.

38. **Metaverse Events**
    Virtual gatherings such as concerts or conferences.
    Example: Travis Scott's Fortnite concert drew millions of attendees.

39. **Metaverse Platforms**
    Virtual ecosystems enabling user interaction and creation.
    Example: Sandbox allows users to build and monetise virtual worlds.

40. **Microtransactions**
    Small digital payments for in-game or online purchases.
    Example: Players buy cosmetic skins in Apex Legends via microtransactions.

41. **Mixed Reality (MR)**
    Combines AR and VR to merge physical and digital worlds.
    Example: Microsoft HoloLens is a popular MR device.

42. **Mobile Wallet**
    A digital wallet accessible through a smartphone.
    Example: Trust Wallet supports multiple cryptocurrencies.

43. **Network Node**
    A participant in a blockchain network.
    Example: Bitcoin miners operate as network nodes.

44. **NFT (Non-Fungible Token)**
    Unique digital assets representing ownership of items like art or virtual real estate.
    Example: Bored Ape Yacht Club NFTs are highly sought-after.

45. **Off-Chain Transactions**
    Transactions processed outside the blockchain for efficiency.
    Example: Lightning Network processes Bitcoin off-chain payments.

46. **Open Source**
Software with publicly available source code.
Example: OpenSea is an open-source NFT marketplace.

47. **Peer-to-Peer (P2P)**
Direct transactions between users without intermediaries.
Example: Filecoin facilitates P2P file sharing.

48. **Permissioned Blockchain**
A blockchain requiring authorisation to participate.
Example: Hyperledger is a permissioned blockchain for enterprises.

49. **Permissionless Blockchain**
Open blockchain accessible to anyone.
Example: Bitcoin is a permissionless network.

50. **Play-to-Earn (P2E)**
Games where players earn cryptocurrency or NFTs.
Example: Axie Infinity rewards players with SLP tokens.

51. **Privacy in the Metaverse**
Ensuring user data is protected in virtual environments.
Example: Privacy-preserving protocols like Zcash aid Metaverse platforms.

52. **Proof of Ownership**
Verification of digital asset ownership via blockchain.
Example: NFTs on OpenSea prove unique ownership.

53. **Public Key**
A cryptographic code used to receive digital assets.
Example: Bitcoin wallets display a public key for transactions.

54. **Reputation System**
Mechanism for establishing trust within a network.
Example: eBay uses a reputation system for sellers.

55. **Scalability**
    The capacity of a system to handle increasing usage.
    Example: Ethereum 2.0 focuses on improving scalability.

56. **Self-Sovereign Identity**
    A decentralised identity owned and controlled by an individual.
    Example: Sovrin Foundation develops self-sovereign identity systems.

57. **Smart Cities**
    Urban areas integrated with digital technologies for efficiency.
    Example: London's smart city initiatives leverage IoT.

58. **Smart Contracts**
    Self-executing contracts with terms directly written into code.
    Example: DeFi platforms like Uniswap use smart contracts.

59. **Spatial Computing**
    Technology enabling interaction between physical and virtual spaces.
    Example: Niantic's Lightship platform enables spatial AR games.

60. **Stablecoin**
    Cryptocurrency pegged to stable assets like fiat currencies.
    Example: USDC is a widely used stablecoin.

61. **Token**
    A digital representation of value on a blockchain.
    Example: Ethereum's ERC-20 tokens are a popular standard.

62. **Token Gating**
    Restricting access based on token ownership.
    Example: Certain Discord communities use token gating for exclusivity.

63. **Tokenomics**
    The economic structure of a cryptocurrency or token.
    Example: Axie Infinity's SLP token is integral to its ecosystem.

64. **Transaction Fee**
    A fee paid to process blockchain transactions.
    Example: Gas fees are paid on Ethereum for each transaction.

65. **Trustless Systems**
    Systems operating without needing user trust.
    Example: Decentralised exchanges like PancakeSwap are trustless.

66. **User-Generated Content (UGC)**
    Content created by users within digital platforms.
    Example: Roblox thrives on UGC from its players.

67. **Utility Token**
    Tokens providing access to services within a blockchain ecosystem.
    Example: BAT tokens are used on the Brave browser.

68. **Virtual Avatars**
    Personalised 3D representations of users.
    Example: Zepeto is popular for creating avatars.

69. **Virtual Collaboration**
    Working together in virtual environments.
    Example: Teams use Spatial for virtual meetings in 3D spaces.

70. **Virtual Concerts**
    Musical performances held in digital spaces.
    Example: Ariana Grande's Fortnite concert was a Metaverse milestone.

71. **Virtual Economy**
    An economic system within virtual environments.
    Example: Fortnite's V-Bucks currency powers its economy.

72. **Virtual Fashion**
    Digital clothing for avatars or AR/VR environments.
    Example: Gucci released virtual sneakers for Metaverse platforms.

73. **Virtual Goods**
    Digital items purchased or earned within virtual spaces.
    Example: Skins in Fortnite are highly popular virtual goods.

74. **Virtual Identity**
    Representation of oneself in digital realms.
    Example: ENS domains provide blockchain-based identities.

75. **Virtual Land**
    Digital real estate within the Metaverse.
    Example: Parcels in Decentraland have sold for millions.

76. **Virtual Marketplace**
    Platforms for trading virtual and digital goods.
    Example: Decentraland has an in-built NFT marketplace.

77. **Virtual Office**
    A workspace within the Metaverse.
    Example: Meta's Horizon Workrooms support virtual office setups.

78. **Virtual Reality (VR)**
    An immersive digital experience via devices like VR headsets.
    Example: Oculus Quest 3 offers advanced VR gaming.

79. **Volatility**
    Rapid changes in the value of digital currencies.
    Example: Bitcoin's price volatility is often discussed in

financial circles.

80. **Wearable Devices**
Technology worn by users for interaction or data collection.
Example: Apple Watch integrates AR experiences.

81. **Web 2.0**
The second generation of the internet focused on user-generated content.
Example: Social media platforms like Facebook define Web 2.0.

82. **Web3**
The next-generation internet focusing on decentralisation and user ownership.
Example: Brave Browser rewards users with Basic Attention Tokens (BAT).

83. **Web3 Wallet**
Digital wallets used for blockchain interactions.
Example: MetaMask supports multiple blockchains for Web3 interactions.

84. **White Paper**
An official document explaining a technology or project.
Example: Satoshi Nakamoto's white paper introduced Bitcoin.

85. **XR (Extended Reality)**
A collective term that encompasses Augmented Reality (AR), Virtual Reality (VR), and Mixed Reality (MR) technologies.
Example: Apple's Vision Pro aims to redefine XR experiences.

86. **Yield Farming**
Earning rewards by lending or staking cryptocurrencies.
Example: Users earn tokens through yield farming on PancakeSwap.

87. **Zero-Knowledge Proof (ZKP)**
    A cryptographic method to prove truth without revealing data.
    Example: zk-SNARKs power Zcash's privacy features.

88. **Algorithmic Stablecoin**
    A type of stablecoin maintained by algorithms rather than reserves.
    Example: Terra's UST was an algorithmic stablecoin.

89. **Beacon Chain**
    The foundational chain in Ethereum's transition to Proof of Stake.
    Example: Ethereum 2.0 uses the Beacon Chain for staking.

90. **Cold Wallet**
    An offline wallet used to securely store cryptocurrencies.
    Example: Ledger and Trezor are popular cold wallets.

91. **Cross-Chain Bridge**
    A tool enabling asset transfers between different blockchains.
    Example: Wormhole connects Solana and Ethereum ecosystems.

92. **Decentralised Storage**
    Storing data across multiple nodes for security and redundancy.
    Example: IPFS and Arweave are decentralised storage solutions.

93. **Dynamic NFTs**
    NFTs that can change based on external conditions or inputs.
    Example: Chainlink enables dynamic NFTs for real-world integrations.

94. **Gasless Transactions**
    Blockchain transactions where fees are covered by another party.

Example: dApps like OpenSea offer gasless NFT listings.

95. **Hardware Wallet**
A physical device used to store cryptocurrencies securely.
Example: A Ledger Nano X is a common hardware wallet.

96. **Minting**
The process of creating a new token or NFT on the blockchain.
Example: Creators mint NFTs on platforms like OpenSea.

97. **Off-Chain Governance**
Decision-making processes that occur outside the blockchain.
Example: Many DAOs use off-chain voting mechanisms.

98. **Pseudonymous Identity**
An identity based on pseudonyms rather than real names.
Example: Blockchain addresses enable pseudonymous transactions.

99. **Sharding**
A blockchain scaling method dividing the network into smaller partitions.
Example: Ethereum 2.0 will implement sharding for scalability.

100. **Tokenised Real Estate**
Real estate assets represented as tokens on a blockchain.
Example: Platforms like Propy allow for tokenised real estate transactions.

101. **Validator**
A participant in Proof of Stake blockchains that validates transactions.
Example: Validators earn rewards for securing the Ethereum network.

About the Authors

Mr. Kalyanjit Hatibaruah is the **Chairman of Flugelsoft Group**, leading a portfolio of companies specialising in various tech and management domains. Holding a BTech degree in Electronics & Communication from NIT Kurukshetra, Haryana, and an MBA from Pune University, he possesses a robust academic foundation complemented by extensive experience in technology stacks, including Ecommerce, Distributed Applications, AI/ML, and Web3. Recognised as a pioneer in Blockchain Applications, he serves as an adviser and leads tech teams on financial projects involving Blockchain and Tokenisation.

An accomplished technology management professional with diverse experience in technology and consulting across multidisciplinary domains, Mr. Hatibaruah is also a renowned public speaker. He frequently addresses topics such as **Web3, Metaverse, Artificial Intelligence, Entrepreneurship, Start-up Ecosystems, and Angel Investing** at business schools, universities, and corporate events.

A committed mentor and investor, Mr. Hatibaruah is an **Angel Investor** with Mumbai Angels and collaborates with numerous start-up incubators and accelerators as a mentor. He is actively involved in incubation programmes at STPI (Gurgaon & Pune), T-Hub, India Accelerator, Jagriti Enterprise Centre Purvanchal (Deoria), and European incubators, particularly focusing on Web3, AI, Metaverse, Blockchain, and emerging technologies. He also invests in start-ups, guiding them in incubation and go-to-market strategies.

His contributions to education and innovation include conducting workshops and offering courses—both online and offline—across diverse topics, including university-level programmes. He was a **Judge at the Smart India Hackathon** 2022-2023 for the Hardware and Software Edition under the Ministry of Education, Government of India. Additionally, he frequently serves as a Judge for national and international hackathons, including the India International Science Festival, and is invited to prestigious events hosted by universities such as IITs, IIMs, and AIIMS.

As a podcast host, Mr. Hatibaruah runs "**Web3 Unleashed**" in partnership with Pod One Entertainment, available on major podcast platforms. His thought leadership extends to mentoring professionals, students, and start-ups to successfully enter and thrive in various industries, offering invaluable guidance on leveraging emerging technologies.

A visionary with a global network, Mr. Hatibaruah maintains strong connections with venture capitalists and professionals across diverse fields. His extensive knowledge and industry experience make him a sought-after resource for those seeking to explore or excel in technology, management, and innovation.

Connect with Kalyanjit Hatibaruah on social media:

Linkedin: linkedin.com/in/kalyanjit
Facebook: facebook.com/kalyanjit

About the Authors

Pratibha Das Hatibaruah is a seasoned technology **entrepreneur and founder of Flugelsoft**, a leading Web3 company specialising in Blockchain, Metaverse, and AI. With 24+ years of experience, she has led innovative product development teams and advised start-ups, earning recognition as an influencer in the Web3 space.

Her extensive experience in technical writing has honed her ability to break down complex technological concepts into accessible, user-friendly content. As a Content Specialist, she has spearheaded diverse projects, leading teams of technical writers, designers, and digital marketers to produce high-quality documentation across multiple verticals, including user manuals, white papers, API documentation, and more.

Certified as a **Microsoft Certified System Engineer (MCSE)** and **Cisco Certified Network Associate (CCNA)**, Pratibha began her career as a Network Engineer at top MNCs like Toyota Kirloskar Motors and Infosys, Bengaluru, before transitioning into entrepreneurship.

Pratibha hosts her **podcast channel,** PRATIBHA'S TECHTALK, where she delves into Web3 technologies and their impact on industries.

She has also created educational content for the Web3 space on **Udemy** and produces videos for her **YouTube channel**, PRATIBHA'S TECHTALK ON METAVERSE.

Her dynamic presence extends to international conferences and universities as an **industry speaker.** She has delivered talks at esteemed venues, including IIT Guwahati, Tura University, J.C. Bose University of Science & Technology, YMCA Faridabad, Assam Engineering Institute (AEI), Marathwada Mitra Mandal's College of Engineering Pune, and Srimad Andavan Arts and Science College, Trichy, among many others.

Pratibha is also a **business mentor**, guiding start-ups and entrepreneurs in the northeast region of India through programmes such as Jagriti Enterprise Centre Purvanchal (JECP) and Tejaswini (an initiative of the Women's Cell, Industries & Commerce Department, Government of Assam, in collaboration with NEHHDC), alongside several other regional and national initiatives aimed at fostering entrepreneurship and innovation.

As an avid **tech blogger**, Pratibha shares insights on her blog, PRATIBHA'S TECH TALK and contributes to global platforms such as *Medium*, *Momspresso*, THUMBPRINT, TWIST AND TWAIN, and BLASTING NEWS. She has also written for national publications like THE ASSAM TRIBUNE and ARUNACHAL24, covering technology, digital marketing, lifestyle, and industry writing.

Though her career is largely defined by technology and entrepreneurship, Pratibha leads a "double life" as a novelist. Under the pen name PRATIBHA R DH, she has authored seven fiction books, including CHILD OF PARADISE (LISTEN TO YOUR DREAMS), a paranormal crime mystery, and BUTTERFLIES IN THE STORM, a romantic suspense novel—both **Amazon bestsellers**. Balancing these contrasting domains is challenging, but her passion for both keeps her journey dynamic and fulfilling.

Connect with Pratibha Das Hatibaruah on social media:

Linkedin: linkedin.com/in/web3pratibha
Facebook: facebook.com/BlockchainEntrepreneurr
Instagram(Tech Channel): instagram.com/pratibha_blockchain_techie
Instagram (Fiction Author): instagram.com/author.pratibha
Blog: pratibhastechtalk.wordpress.com

www.ingramcontent.com/pod-product-compliance
Ingram Content Group UK Ltd.
Pitfield, Milton Keynes, MK11 3LW, UK
UKHW021406190726
13845UKWH00028B/923

9 789334 179118